Laurie Green studied in London and New York before working in Birmingham for twenty years both in parish ministry and theological education. He then returned to his native east London as Team Rector of Poplar. Now Bishop of Bradwell in Essex, he works with urban, rural and suburban communities. His books include *Power to the Powerless* (a *Church Times* Book of the Year), *Let's Do Theology* (Continuum), and *The Impact of the Global* (Board of Social Responsibility).

Urban Ministry
and the
Kingdom of God

Laurie Green

First published in Great Britain in 2003 by
Society for Promoting Christian Knowledge
Holy Trinity Church
Marylebone Road
London NW1 4DU

British Library Cataloguing-in-Publication Data
A catalogue record for this book is available from the British Library

ISBN 0-281-05530-0

10 9 8 7 6 5 4 3 2 1

Designed and typeset by Kenneth Burnley, Wirral, Cheshire
Printed in Great Britain by MPG Books, Bodmin, Cornwall

Contents

This book is affectionately dedicated to
Nadir Dinshaw, Geoffrey Harper and John Vincent,
dear friends and mentors

The Structure of this Book

All theology has a context and it is therefore of utmost importance that we acknowledge our context or incarnation, and do our theologizing accordingly. Many theologians find that idea very challenging, apparently thinking that when they do theology they somehow become disembodied spirits. Some proclaim themselves to be doing 'contextual theology' when in fact all they do is look at their context and then draw abstract conclusions about it. I want to be much more ambitious for theology than that.

In an earlier book, *Let's Do Theology*, I describe contextual theology as the dynamic interaction of four elements, and that is why this book has a fourfold shape. It seems to me that the first requirement of contextual theology, and therefore its first element, has to be an acknowledgement of where we are, and to whom we belong. And so the first part of this book seeks to tell the story of our urban context here in the UK and the place the Christian Church has within that. While that first element might be described as a 'story-telling' phase of theology, the second element of a properly contextual theology requires that we look more objectively and analytically at our situation so that we can discern the values which underlie our present urban context and name the issues that emerge. The second part of this book therefore looks intently at our present urban situation in the light of more recent learning and experience, drawing out the values and meanings of our urban culture. Third is that element of theology which we usually call 'theological reflection'. The third part of the book therefore tries to draw together all that has gone before – our story, and our analysis – and reflects upon all that in the light of the Gospels and the story they tell us of Jesus of Nazareth. His central focus upon the Kingdom of God leads us particularly to reflect in this book on how the Kingdom principles shed light on our present urban predicament. Finally, the fourth element of 'doing theology' demands contextual response, and so the fourth part of the book asks how we should respond to the delights and challenges of our urban world in the light of our analysis and theological reflection. We describe what the key features of a Kingdom-based urban ministry and mission might be.

The book therefore divides into four parts, derived from that fourfold understanding of how contextual theology functions, although even within each chapter the interplay of these four elements can be discerned. To help the reader to see where each chapter locates in this fourfold cycle of 'doing theology', it may be useful to glance from time to time at the Contents page of the book, although I hope that the book's shape will feel quite natural, especially to those accustomed to the processes of contextual theology.

Acknowledgements

I owe a debt of gratitude to those who have helped in the development of this book, not least to Michael Fox, David Eaton and Andrew Davey who read early drafts, to Ruth McCurry at SPCK for her encouragement, and to Pat Howes who helped with some of the typing. The book was written while recovering from two stays at St Luke's Hospital in London, so I do thank the surgeons and staff for all their care – without which the book would never have been finished.

Part 1

Telling the Urban Story

The British urban context and the place of the Christian Church in that story

1 | Welcome to an Urban Life

Deep within the East End of London, my mother lives in the terraced house in which I was born and in which I lived the first seventeen years of my life. I return often, for my present home is not too far distant. My memories of my inner-city childhood some forty years ago are in sharp contrast with much of what my mother is now experiencing and yet, in so many deeper ways, much remains the same. I grew up in the period just following the Second World War, when the East End was an ideal playground for boisterous children like us. The bomb sites were exciting places for discovery and fantasy games, the roads were sufficiently clear of traffic to allow for gangs of children to race from one end to the other in pursuit of a ball, and rock and roll was just beginning to change the face of music. Parents were pleased to be home from the war or welcomed the cessation of the perpetual bombing, and although rationing kept them down at heel, there was the promise of a future with steady work and even the chance of one day owning your own TV. There was a strict code of Victorian values, harshly maintained: the men knew their place and the women made the family decisions. Our extended family was all around us in the adjacent houses or further into the city where some had not been bombed during the blitz. The local council was firmly in the hands of the Labour Party and, as they spent vast sums on education, even if like me you didn't pass your 11+ exam first time, there was a chance that you would be given a place at the grammar school where you would be expected to study hard for the benefit of the community's future. It was a very poor but exciting world.[1]

My family had strong Communist Party leanings but were not ill-disposed towards the parish church. The church was liberal catholic by inclination and the Vicar, Nigel Porter, took a strong radical stand on most matters of political and theological significance. The social life of the parish church was vibrant, like the family life of the community which surrounded it, and the people of the parish were usually white, hard-working, in-your-face cockneys who were determined to get their lives back together after the vicissitudes of war. By the time I came to look for my first evening job at the age of thirteen, it was with a Jewish barber, David Firestone. Most of the local shops were Jewish-run, but the Jewish community had not had an easy time in the East End even though by the 1950s things were a lot easier. My aunt remembers as a child being put up on to the back of an open lorry for safety while my grandmother helped to fight the police who were protecting Sir Oswald Mosley's Fascists who intended to rid the East End of its Jewish community. That was the 1936 Battle of Cable Street. The poky rooms over the barber's shop afforded accommodation for the others who worked in the shop. I was grateful to Ed, a Canadian, for teaching me my first guitar chords and a number of songs which would serve me well in years to come. When David the barber decided to sell up and emigrate to the newly founded state of Israel, I was lucky enough to find new employment at the local jellied-eel factory just along the road from our house. My expectation was that when I left school, I would go to work in the local docks where my father years before had loaded timber and food from around the world. He himself had spent many years before that as a merchant seaman sailing those ships out of the London docks to ports across the world, as far as Africa and Asia and then across to the Americas. After lorry-driving and a few spells of unemployment, he was pleased to find a job driving London buses, while my mother continued at the factory, and so both found themselves increasingly working alongside people of various ethnic backgrounds, who were by now becoming a more visible presence in the community. The Jewish and Irish migrants were now joined by families from the Caribbean and later still by Asian refugees who were being thrown out of Uganda by the dictator Idi Amin. I, meanwhile, had gone to work in East Ham market on my grandmother's jewellery stall, and it was noticeable there how the market traders were having to adjust to the swiftly changing tastes of the new clientele. So it was that even our small part of the city continued to experience, as all vibrant cities do, the rich interplay of cultures and effects of events around the world.

The new wave of immigration had brought into the area very large numbers of Asian people but they had no temples, gurdwaras and mosques in which to worship. The white community was already moving out to the surrounding suburbs and council estates, so the number of local worshipping Christians was declining rapidly. They therefore decided that they would sell their large church hall at a reduced rate to the local Sikhs as a community and worship centre. The church appointed a full-time worker to learn more about the new incoming Asian community and to help build bridges. It was a courageous move, but one not welcomed by all. Some felt that the church's task was to care for the white community and not the new incomers. The new Sikh gurdwara actually did attract more Sikhs into the community and often the local streets were gridlocked with worshippers who had come from all over London to worship. More recently however, the church congregation has found its numbers increasing once again, this time because of the arrival of substantial numbers of African Christians into the area. The new parish priest is himself Nigerian and a wonderfully generous pastor. The worship has once again become more vibrant, and the future looks exciting and promising.

However, the original white community, proud of its working-class heritage, felt pushed aside by the incoming cultures, while a new breed of liberal politician and powerful local business interests only served to alienate them further. The Alf Garnett mentality, mouthing off against the 'Pakis and the blacks', vented the raw anger engendered by this sense of marginalization, and the area proved to be an ideal breeding ground for the British National Party and like-minded fascists who found themselves gaining at least superficial support. The segregation of the various communities, even within the same locality, did not help to alleviate the antagonisms, and the church's community worker had plenty to do as she sought to interpret one community to another.

But, for all the nastiness, there was another side to our new multicultural neighbourhood. When my father died in his eighty-seventh year, the local Asian women went from door to door taking a small collection as a gift to my mother in her bereavement, and as we waited for the family to gather before the service, women from the street came out to my mother and wrapped her in warm embraces of support. They could not communicate verbally, but those embraces said more than any words and buoyed up my mother in a shared expression of grief and love. We all walked together along the street from the house to the church in the way that I remembered so well from my childhood. It was as if the history of our working-class cultures had come full circle and met together.

But meeting across the cultures remains rare. My wife runs a parents' and toddlers' club attached to the school where she works, and she tries to create opportunities for the parents to share their stories. Yan was brought up during the Cultural Revolution in China so her parents were expected to give their time to industrial work rather than the family. She was therefore cared for in the communal nursery and so has no memory at all of the sort of family relationships we would take for granted. Rahana is a mother who was born in London but of Bengali parents. She feels herself for all the world to be a British person. And yet, as she takes her tiny children to school, she is fearful of being attacked on the streets since she dresses in the custom of her Bengali family, and that attracts the antagonism of white gangs. Rahana is just so pleased that she has the support of the extended family around her. Jasmine, on the other hand, is a third member of the group. Her great-grandparents came to east London from Jamaica in the 1950s and she has yet to know what a stable family could be. Her partner proved to be unreliable but she has done a wonderful job, bringing up her little girl without any family supports at all. The Toddler Group is a life-line.

My own family had arrived many generations before, to work in the shipyards but my grandfather became the landlord of a notorious east London pub and he saw that, as each new wave of settlers arrived, so earlier communities would move out to make room for them. Many were forced to move because their properties had been designated for slum clearance and the bulldozer. Others hoped to better themselves, while others wanted to move away from an area where their own cockney way of life was becoming a minority culture. Many who left our street at that time went to live in the new housing estates in Essex, or nearer home where new houses and flats were being built on land cleared of slums or bomb damage. Either way, they benefited from new properties, each with hot running water and bath – a New Jerusalem! I remember Uncle Arthur telling us that he had decided to 'get out' and go to live in a high-rise where he could have wonderful views, no more overcrowding, brand-new kitchen and all 'mod cons'. When we recall that in 1961, 50 per cent of all East End households still had no access to a plumbed bath, this was indeed a dream come true. The developers had no thought of consulting those who were destined to live on the new estates about their wishes, of course, but still I remember everyone being very thankful.

The sad fact is that the promise of that 'New Jerusalem' turned sour. Many felt uprooted and forgotten. They had lost access to their extended families, their jobs and their old dependable networks and amenities. Some were consigned to tower blocks that looked for all the world like filing cabinets in which to store old reports and forgotten statistics. Social planning had thrown groups of struggling people all together into a new struggling place, and slowly began to label them as 'a problem' because, since all the designs and plans for these estates had promised so well, it therefore stood to reason that the blame for the souring of the vision should be laid at the door, not of the planners, but of the new tenants.[2]

On closer analysis, however, we can see that many of those outer housing estates were quite literally designed with exclusion in view. Planners thought it would enhance the sense of community if they boxed estates in on themselves, served only by a single road access. But this only made it more difficult to get off the estate at all, so that access to leisure and shopping facilities was almost impossible for those who could not afford a car. Journeys to work were sometimes impossible. Today, these outer estates have all the deprivation of the inner cities, compounded by the isolation and lack of infrastructure normally found in pockets of rural deprivation. Some estates in other parts of the country were built specifically to serve a local mining or production centre, but with the de-industrialization of the Thatcher era, men now unemployed no longer had any reason to leave the estate each day for work and, with the men encroaching upon the women's community systems each day, family life began to crumble under the strain. I served as a curate on an estate in Birmingham, where we ran a youth club for hundreds of skin-head 'punks' who were seeking to find some coherent identity amid the problems of the surrounding community. One of their delights was to 'TWOC' cars – 'take without owner's consent' – and to drive them off the estate until the petrol ran out. Their excitement at getting away from the confines of the estate was only eclipsed by my own anger at having to drive out in the middle of the night to bring them back from distant police stations!

These estates have often been plagued by years of local authority mismanagement which has totally unbalanced communities, leaving the elderly isolated from their families and terrified of the new youth culture which has taken over their streets. With escalating poverty and lack of employment, some estates begin to evidence a dependency culture. At its worst, the professional carers and officers have become dependent upon those they serve for their own sense of worth and even salary, while those receiving care have become adept at working the benefits system and at little else. It is as if there is a conspiracy of dependency.

For some of these estates the promise of the 'New Jerusalem' has lost its sparkle. And yet those who live and minister today on these forgotten estates sense constantly that, despite all expectation, the 'glory' – the presence of God – has certainly not departed. They see God in the birth-giving of the single mum, in the faithful routine of eking out a living, in the fun in the pub on Saturday nights, in the despair of the unemployed youngster, and in the birthday party at the Sunday school. There is an innate goodness in those ordinary local people who are not on the make and who share generously from what little they have. Rowdy youngsters turn out to be longing for someone just to take an interest in them. God is here with us, here on the estate, in all the joys and the sorrows.

But not all estates are in such a mess. Some are better placed, better constructed and closer to those amenities and places of work which make for a viable and enjoyable future. Many of those who left the East End have prospered and moved to those parts of London's eastward sprawl which we would count as 'suburbia' – be they the better quality new estates or the redeveloped and extended towns and villages of Essex. The tentacles of the Underground system reach out from the centre of London to road after road of semi-detached homes dating from as far back as the 1930s, while further afield the constant upgrading of radial roads and commuter rail stations aids the urban sprawl which continues to attract despite phenomenal house price increases and the agonies of commuter travel. All around me in Essex are those, like my now dispersed family of uncles and cousins, who have worked very hard all their lives to attain the suburban dream – a dream with two somewhat opposing strands. The first is a dream of home ownership – a piece of land to call one's own. It is, essentially, a yearning for personal identity, of having 'arrived' after all the struggles of those former generations in the hard-pressed East End. As well as this dream of independence, there is the antithetical suburban yearning which craves community – a nostalgic sense that you can have community without having to work for it – like a wistful episode of *The Archers*. The dishwasher and fridge are hidden away behind country pine panels, and the four-wheel-drive has the air of an up-market Land Rover.

Many suburban people do work very hard, trying to create a sense of community and 'clubbiness' in the suburb, the churches and other associations and friendship circles playing a large part in that endeavour. A lot of energy goes into creating and sustaining this suburban dream, and the modern suburbanite exudes a healthy and sporty image of worldly success and personal togetherness. They have built up and sustained a place, prestige and sufficient possessions – all the reward of hard work and perseverance.

The benefits of living in pleasant surroundings with acceptable schools and facilities cannot be gainsaid but there are tell-tale signs of a disillusionment, a wish for something more. In the past, the suburban churches were full of families who came with thanksgiving in their hearts for the obvious benefits which life had afforded them. Many suburban Christians worked hard for local ecumenicity and the development of evangelism. Some even offered their expertise to their denominational bureaucracies. The 'inner cities' sometimes became quite resentful of this apparent success and spoke of the 'white flight' from the city, issuing in the 'suburban captivity of the Church'.³ Suburban life had its own problems, however, and some Christians felt the strain of struggling on with the ethical compromises of their workplace, the muddles of suburban family life and the guilt of feeling comfortable in an unjust world. Even the suburban physical environment was evidencing signs of stress, with deteriorating community facilities, declining or non-existent local centres, and an overbearing dependence upon the car. Today, the quality of life has begun to deteriorate for some who are into the constant round of commuting on unreliable and overcrowded trains, leaving in the early morning and getting home very late each night. Older folk find it all too much and mark off the days to retirement, while the more energetic young adults often prefer to enjoy the fun of the town or city, and begin to think their monochrome suburb boring in comparison.

Back in the towns and cities, the pavement cafés and bars, cinemas and theatres, clubs, discos and galleries, all offer what no other environment can. But those who prefer to live within easier access of all this vibrant life must be prepared to pay the prices being asked for apartments in the newly 'gentrified' quarters. Many erstwhile suburbanites are nevertheless choosing to live back in the areas their grandparents vacated, because they enjoy the multicultural environment that their grandparents did their utmost to escape. Some churches have learnt to adjust to the cultural needs of this 'new urban gentry', offering worship services with plenty of informational input and well-managed programmes of education and training. A 'can-do' culture appeals to the mind-set, while first-class presentations from speakers and worship leaders attend to the questions of personal spirituality with which this, largely younger, audience is struggling.

In the city areas redundant warehousing and canal or dock-side water frontages have been transformed to accommodate sophisticated leisure facilities for the young people who buzz around the busy city and make it their own. High-flying executives jump taxi-cabs, African pop music mingles with the aroma of fine Italian food and South American coffees, young and old wear the latest styles from around the world, and the old look younger and more energetic as they crowd the evening Underground train for the latest cinema or theatrical event.

Stand on a street corner in today's city and you will see such an array of people. Early in the morning will come the cleaners, often people of colour, then the security workers – men finding it difficult to acquire more lucrative employment after early redundancy. The street then begins to buzz with office workers jumping buses and cars, fast followed by bigger limousines carrying the shakers and movers of the financial district. Tourists wander, couriers screech by on cycles and motorbikes, and coffee bars spill out on to the pavement. People from around the world cruise by in groups, and as the evening draws on and the workers drag themselves home, so a new flurry of life begins, with boozing boys and girls, ritzy lights, clubs and cinemas. As the cold of night draws on, the homeless come dragging their make-shift sleeping bags and their dogs into the shelter of a dirty shop entry. The city is a place of opportunity or squalor, depending upon the level at which you look and live, and the time of day you're on the street – whether you feel you belong or feel alienated from all that the city offers and represents.

For behind the glitzy façade and the togetherness of the 'designer city' lurks the spectre of poverty and fragmentation. For seven years I lived with my young family in Handsworth in Birmingham, one of the most deprived areas of that great city. The poverty was brutal, physical deformity and illness on the streets very evident, drugs and danger loomed everywhere and a heavy-handed police presence alienated the populace. One summer evening in 1985 I attended a public meeting where local people begged the police to adopt a different style. Two days later two young policemen found themselves at the heart of a street confrontation and that night the community erupted into what became known as the Handsworth Riots. Before that event the various ethnic communities were getting along reasonably well with one another, but the next morning the national press reported the uprising as a 'race riot'. From that time on, the atmosphere between the ethnic groups became less trustful and sometimes outwardly hostile, and even those who knew better began to interpret the riots in the same racist terms as those introduced by the media. With such high concentrations of bad housing, unemployment, addictions, crime and poverty, the community was powerless to have its own voice and explanation heard, and began to act out the interpretations which others imposed upon it.

It is difficult to describe the brokenness of some urban areas. There are too many disadvantaged people crammed into the confines of poor housing, deprived of decent medical services, and put upon by inadequately trained and over-stretched social workers. Local government seems out of its depth, schools struggle, local shops close and loan sharks have a field-day. Divergent cultures begin to clash and the homeless poor and asylum seekers are put into local bed-and-breakfast accommodation on the assumption that this sort of area is better able to handle the influx than more wealthy communities. Those who are called to urban ministry, however, soon find all this reminding them that Jesus chose to become the servant and friend of the most deprived and alienated of his contemporaries. The Gospels place people like this at the very heart of the Good News message, and the signs he worked among them were the sacraments of the new age – what Jesus called the 'Kingdom of God'. He made friends of the poor and the downtrodden, but also, in his Sermon on the Mount, even held them up as the major recipients of the blessedness that would follow upon his acts of salvation. These are the people among whom he chose to live and work, and so his Church must be there too.

The urban vocation

At the crossroads and in the side streets of this great kaleidoscope which is our contemporary urban experience, we find church buildings great and small. Some are traditional Victorian gothic, looking past their 'best before' date, while others are in fine condition, welcoming us in to a full programme of concerts and services. Some churches retreat from the world, hidden behind grey crumbling churchyards, while other chapels and halls speak of the revival days of years long past. Some churches are vibrant on Sunday mornings when most folk are in bed, but those same churches look dead later in the day when everyone is up and about. Some sport large, flapping banners across their frontage advertising the latest Alpha course or that 'Your Community Church Meets Here'. Some appeal to a particular ethnic group to come and join people of their own background – services in Swahili or Spanish; others proclaim a certain style – 'Holiness' or 'Pentecostal' or 'Prayer Book Only'. Some offer peace and quiet, while others support various projects for the homeless and needy. Each church tries to respond in its own way to the urban challenge – some with remarkable success, others fearing that they've lost their way, attended by just a few old retainers who are quite unrepresentative of the new urban scene. Some may conclude that there is no 'spiritual' interest left in urban people, but my experience is different. David Tudor, Team Rector of Canvey Island, remarks that people in his parish will very often say to him, 'I'm not religious, vicar, but . . .' Then they ask for a prayer or share a significant spiritual experience from their life's story. There is a deep hidden sense of the presence of God in the place, but how the Church might help that to be expressed is the continuing challenge.

I often meet young women and men who are attracted to urban mission because they sense quite rightly that ministry here can be less cramped than in a big, highly managed suburban church, leaving more scope for imaginative multicultural worship and the excitements of daily church life. There are unlimited opportunities for collaboration with others of goodwill, including secular organizations who are here trying to make the urban scene a good place in which to be. Here they know they will be in touch with all the issues which are crucial to today's world. Here they sense it is possible to serve God's Kingdom in direct and telling ways alongside people who are well aware of their needs and the needs of the community. At the same time they will be surrounded by hidden giftedness, exuberance and resilience amid the harsh realities of human living. People from all around the world, the rich and powerful, the poor and oppressed, all live within a short journey, and in the church community many will be found worshipping, witnessing, working and playing alongside one another. Without the clutter of doctrinal complexity or nicety, here are people bundled together who can come at the New Testament with a freshness, wanting to walk the walk, not just talk the talk. If you want life to the full, this is a fine place in which to be a Christian minister, ordained or lay.

By the time I left school I had become a committed Christian, so went off to live in a religious commune in Balsall Heath, then a red-light district of Birmingham. I later returned to the East End so that I could attend London University before ordination. In all I have lived some fifty years of my life in heavily urbanized localities in such cities as London, Birmingham and New York, and the chance to do urban theology with others and to engage with them in urban life and ministry excites me still. That's why this book exists – as an invitation to others to enjoy something of the delight and challenge of what I have found to be a wonderful and fulfilling vocation. I do not purport to be anything of an expert, and much of what I share in these pages derives from the wisdom of others who have helped me and shown me the way.

It was in 1890 that Henry M. Stanley published his best-seller, *In Darkest Africa: the Way In*. It told of the missionary adventures of Dr Livingstone, but it led William Booth to publish in the very same year his riposte, *In Darkest England: the Way Out*, as a challenge to the English people to look to the mission field in its midst. 'May we not find a parallel at our own doors,' asked Booth, 'and discover within a stone's throw of our cathedrals and palaces similar horrors to those which Stanley has found existing in the great Equatorial forest?' Today, the adventure is still on our doorstep. But it is not just horror that we'll find in our contemporary urban scene. I remember one occasion when I was leading a study group of East Enders, we began sharing with one another memories of our earlier lives. As we shared those memories I was numbed into silence on hearing such horrific stories, because in urban areas it is often the case that people cannot think about their lives without despair and pain beyond bearing. Yet these same people often seem so vibrant, carefree, bombastic and ebullient. Wonderful friendships and unaffected fun abound. Television soap operas and all the statistics in the world cannot do it justice, because so much of the reality of urban people lies hidden. One senses God's pain, but also, and often inextricably linked, we know too God's joy in its midst. In my own east London, it's our custom to have very elaborate funerals with black-plumed horses and masses of flowers. Most ministers today will ask the bereaved family to choose a piece of appropriate music to be played at the ceremony, so it was little wonder when Charlie died that the family asked that we should sing the West Ham Football Club anthem, 'I'm Forever Blowing Bubbles'. We sang the song with tears streaming down our cheeks, the words summing up something of what it is to be a person of faith amid the harsh realities of East End life. 'Fortune's always hiding; I've looked everywhere. I'm forever blowing bubbles, pretty bubbles in the air.' If we had been living elsewhere we might have been singing, 'Walk on through the wind, walk on through the rain. Walk on with love in your heart, and you'll never walk alone.' These words, when sung by those for whom they are dear, give expression to something which is much deeper than the casual observer will realize.[4]

A tough urban context affects the understanding people have of the God they may occasionally give assent to. George, who had been coming to the annual Remembrance Day Service for years, would say to me, 'God is good, God is good.' Despite the torture of life, he senses the presence of God as a loving protector in heaven who in the end will make all things well. At the other end of the spectrum, under the pressure of misfortune, some will bitterly resent the Father God in whom they still believe. On a tombstone in my old graveyard in Poplar someone had scratched with a heavy crayon, 'God is a bastard'. As I reflected on that, I could only turn over and over in my mind Christ's words, 'My God, my God, why hast thou forsaken me?' But for many, there is also a God of last resort. Someone may say, 'We are at such a loss and so unprotected here that if we do not have faith then what are we left with?' My Stalinist grandmother, who had suffered poverty beyond imagining, would say, 'If there wasn't a God, Laurie, there wouldn't be nothing. Not just nothing, but not even nothing.'

I hazard to suggest that there are corrupted remnants of a trinitarian theology lurking here. For many, God the Father is the judging teacher.

There are many who live the tough urban experience with no loving father around the home anyway, so father as judge is about right in their experience. The loving protector God on the other hand is there in the figure of Jesus, the one who knows crucifixion and yet has the power to save. And the God of last resort, who has simply got to be there, may reflect an old belief in God the Holy Spirit. It seems that these contorted vestiges of Christian doctrine are still in the inherited language and folk religion of some urban people. But even more important is the felt experience of the presence of God which remains at those deep but rarely expressed levels: 'I'm not religious, but . . .'

It is the figure of Jesus himself which resonates most strongly with people in these harshest of urban environments. They understand what it means to be born in a stable and they are impressed with a man who comes knowingly to the city and who works to remove injustice and suffering – and where that proves to be impossible they see him take that suffering and transfigure it so that it becomes the raw material for divine love. They love his rugged determination and they know from experience just how overwhelming the powers are that are stacked against him. In Poplar we could always rely on a full church on Good Friday when we enacted the story of his sufferings and looked to the cross as the gateway to resurrection. They could all answer 'Yes' when we sang 'Were you there when they crucified my Lord?'

But while all this is being experienced in the back streets of so many forgotten inner-city neighbourhoods, any raw recruit coming from theological college who has been trained to expect only deprivation and poverty in the city is in for a big surprise! In the parish of Poplar which I served, on one side of the East India Dock Road there were high-rise concrete buildings whose stairwells and corridors stank of urine and poverty, but on the other, new buildings were rising into the heavens which spoke of brash elegance and obscene wealth. Lorded over by the Canary Wharf Tower, still the tallest in the land, international money-market financiers meet media tycoons and property developers over sumptuous lunches. The old dockside warehouses have become luxury studio apartments for the rich businessmen and women who keep the wheels of global trade and finance turning. This too is the East End of London!

I now live in a countryside suburb along the Thames Estuary, but the government has just designated this locality its number one regeneration project, so the city of London begins to encroach upon areas that have always lived in the shadow of the great metropolis, but are now seeing their future totally geared to it. New infrastructural building is already kicking up cement dust and gridlocking our local roads. And this is a story multiplied across the country, with towns and cities everywhere clamouring for their own slice of the regeneration cake. Our cities are undergoing major plastic surgery as vast investments are made in their built environment in the hope of attracting the commerce and enterprise of this new international 'urban renaissance'.

And this of course is only to mention the changes in the *built* environment that regeneration is promising. Regionalization, Development Agencies and a plethora of New Deals, Action Zones and Neighbourhood Renewal Areas are all part of the national government's urban programme for social renewal to stand alongside the regeneration of the built environment. And in all these schemes and proposals the repeated watchword is 'partnership'. Government policy papers are produced which challenge the 'faith communities' to be involved alongside the corporate and voluntary sectors, to play our part in this holistic planning and development.[5] But does the Church have a ready strategy in order to offer its distinctive contribution to this urban challenge? For if all this continues to go ahead on the basis that regeneration has no spiritual dimension, I fear for the future of our nation.

An urban gospel?

What then is the gospel – the Good News – for men and women, boys and girls, in this new urban age? For urban age it certainly is. Britain has been for generations an urbanized and urbanizing nation. Ever since vast numbers of people moved to the towns and cities during the industrial revolution, Britain has continued to urbanize, so that now most of its population lives in cities, towns and suburbs. By 1950 over 82 per cent of the population of the UK was considered urban, and that proportion is now increasing to over 90 per cent, with only 5 per cent specifically rural. The cultural history of the UK teaches us, however, that the English have always harboured a strong anti-urban streak and most commentators admit that we British have never been very good at the urban. D. H. Lawrence observed that 'The English are town-birds through and through, today, as the inevitable result of complete industrialisation. Yet they don't know how to build a city, how to think of one, or how to live in one. They are all suburban, pseudo-cottagey, and not one of them knows how to be truly urban.'[6] Victorian literature is full of anxiety about the loss of the rural idyll, and when Ebenezer Howard[7] drew up his great plan to house the masses in 1898, his vision of a 'Garden City' with large parks, gardens and allotments sought to return the urban population to as near a rural lifestyle as he could contrive.

It might be said that, apart from the occasional flutter, the Church too has been reluctant to give its whole heart to British urbanization. Perhaps we sense that answers to urban problems have, by and large, eluded governments through the years and we are loath to commit ourselves to an urban programme where we too may stand little chance of outward success. Will long-term investment of resources in vulnerable and poor urban areas really pay dividends which can sustain a national Church which is increasingly dependent upon the giving of its congregational members? Could it be more sensible to concentrate on suburban areas where the Church has a tradition of strength and sustainability? Sometimes a local church has gone in with an urban local authority and built a large community church centre, only to be left holding the baby when the political climate has changed and the local authority has pulled out! While the Church knows it has a duty to these poor areas and is also concerned to deliver on its parish vision of a presence in every community, in the marginalized rural and urban areas alike there is a reducing probability of being able to sustain that parochial presence, given our present strategies and financial strictures.

Despite the pragmatic and historical pressures upon us to withdraw resources from the poor urban parishes, a Church with a vibrant theology and a proper sense of God's call for justice is bound nevertheless to face the challenge and stay in the areas where the majority of Britain's population live. The very compact and concentrated nature of our city, town and housing estate environments means that they are often the places where the most crucial theological issues of our age become clearly focused. It is here that issues of identity and difference, power and powerlessness, global and local, inclusion and exclusion, place and sustainability, are writ large. It is here that questions of success, power, weakness, crucifixion and resurrection are explored moment by moment.

On the pavements and in the tenement blocks of poor urban landscapes, one meets the Jesus of the Gospels at every turn, and our congregations witness that fact daily. At the other extreme, the creators of wealth are here – those who generate and maintain the British economy, still at least the fourth largest economy in the world. From our towns and cities they manage and direct the lives of countless millions around the globe. Here too are the opinion-formers, working within the media, entertainment and advertising industries. Bankers, bureaucrats, politicians – all grapple daily with some of the biggest issues and most powerful forces that shape our world. And they all need to hear the challenge and the wisdom of the gospel.

This book calls the Church to a renewed vocation for our urban mission today. We rejoice that so much is already being achieved, but a great deal has been happening recently, both globally and nationally, which presents radically new challenges and which may therefore require innovative urban mission responses. We are the heirs of a rich and brave heritage of urban mission, ministry and theology, but recent strides have been made in biblical scholarship and in urban studies which provide us with new tools for our endeavour. The challenge is to celebrate our towns, cities and estates and transform the urban experience, that it may become for all an exciting and vibrant experience of fulfilment, choice, happiness and justice. That will be Good News indeed – gospel for an increasingly urban Britain.

2 | Telling the Urban Story

Each discipline has its own way of describing and appreciating the urban scene, and we who would offer an urban ministry do well to attend to the insights which these disciplines bring and to the great variety of ways in which they tell the urban story. We can begin with a brief overview of the way the Bible views the urban landscape.

The biblical city

It should come as no surprise to us that the city is writ large across the pages of the Bible. In Luke's Gospel we are told that as Jesus 'came near and saw the city, he wept over it' (Luke 19.41, NRSV) – and those tears alone are sufficient justification for our concentration on urban mission. Luke further tells us that as the final conflict of Jesus' ministry became more focused so 'he resolutely turned his face towards Jerusalem' (Luke 9.51), and all the Gospels register that the final days of his life were centred upon that capital city. It was there that the ultimate expression of love would be enacted on the cross and the salvation of the world ensured. Time and again in the Bible God uses the urban setting to enact the divine programme of salvation.

God's pain and God's delight

The book of Genesis tells how Cain, on leaving the security of God's presence, builds Enoch, the first city, as a defence and sanctuary against the hostile and chaotic world around him. It is there that both technology and the arts are first developed, but as the Genesis saga unfolds, the people use those gifts to build the Tower of Babel – 'Come, let us build ourselves a city, and a tower with its top in the heavens, and let us make a name for ourselves.' Their city is a symbol of their power, and their common language an indication of the global reach of their communication technology. Much to their surprise, it does not last.

The patriarch Abraham is living in the city of Ur in Mesopotamia, a shrine city of over 200 acres supported by an infrastructure of canals, harbours, and of course its shrine temple, or ziggurat tower, reaching up to heaven. Abram is called to leave Ur, that city of self-aggrandizement, and journey in search of a land where God's glory alone would be proclaimed. The letter to the Hebrews later describes Abraham's journey of faith in the following terms: 'He looked forward to the well-founded city, designed and built by God' (Hebrews 11.10).

This biblical ambivalence towards urban life resonates with our own experience. We too seek the beautiful city, even though much of our urban experience is so discouraging. The city promises relationships of security, justice and sharing, and yet we constantly fail to attain that promise, and experience instead urban violence, injustice and deprivation. I am arrested by the words of that contemporary prophet, Jürgen Moltmann, when he says, 'We are not theologians because we are religious; we are theologians because in the face of this world we miss God. We are crying out for his righteousness and justice and are not prepared to come to terms with mass death on earth.' But having bemoaned the negative, he then goes on to say:

> But for me theology also springs from God's love for life – the love for life that we experience in the presence of the life-giving Spirit and that enables us to move beyond our resignation and begin to love life here and now. These are also Christ's two experiences of God: the kingdom of God and the cross, and because of that they are the foundations of christian theology as well: God's delight and God's pain. It is out of the tension between these two that hope is born for the kingdom in which God is wholly in the world and the world is wholly in God.[1]

The Bible's ambivalence about the city reveals the promise and the pain which God shares with us as we go about our human endeavour of living out the godly society, the Kingdom of God, in an increasingly urbanized world.

Freed from Egyptian captivity, the Hebrew tribes cross the Jordan river and take the cities of Canaan. These primitive capital cities, named as consorts to the Ba'al gods, were ruled over by local princeling warlords. But as each city fell to the invading tribes, so the Promised Land became theirs and the cities sanctified. It is difficult to overestimate just how significant the Land thus became in the hearts and minds of the Jewish people once this settlement had taken place. And as their history unfolded, so the cities of the Promised Land and their stories became tales of God's dealings with them as a people. When they were close to God, then God's justice and generosity were revealed in the city. But when evil and injustice ruled the city then, said the prophets, they could expect dire consequences from the Lord. So it was that God's pain and God's delight were ever present with them in the city.

When the Hebrew people called upon the prophet Samuel to give them a king like the nations around them (1 Samuel 8—9) all these reservations were bound to surface. To retain a dispersed rural federation of tribes would, some believed, guard against the sin of Babel and continue the recognition of God as the only legitimate authority for a godly people. King David very cleverly sought to sway the mind of the anti-urbanites by taking the ark of the covenant itself, the symbol of God's presence, to reside in the city that he had captured (2 Samuel 6) so that Jerusalem would no longer be merely the political capital but the very residence of Godhead – the Holy City.

Even so, throughout the long history of kingship in Israel and Judah the ambiguity of the city continues to inform the biblical story. God looked for 'fair judgement, but found injustice, uprightness (*tsedaqah*), but found cries of distress (*tse'aqah*)' (Isaiah 5.7). God's anguished judgement and God's continuing promise strive in tension throughout the long period of the monarchy, and in the end it is Israel's failure to live out an urban holiness that results in the fall of Jerusalem and the banishment into exile of the people of the Promise.

So it is that the people of Israel find themselves as urban refugees in the great city of Babylon, itself the imperial centre of a network of urban centres of control and subjugation – the city which will become the biblical epitome of all that is evil about urban life. Yet it is here in Babylon that the prophet Jeremiah exhorts the subjugated Jewish exiles to 'build houses, settle down; plant gardens and eat what they produce . . . work for the good of the city to which I have exiled you; pray to Yahweh on its behalf, since on its welfare yours depends' (Jeremiah 29.5–7, NJB). Even amid these dire circumstances God's hope and promise for the city are never allowed to diminish but remain a central feature of the divine strategy.

When at last these urban refugees return from exile, it is Nehemiah, the archetypal urban developer, who rebuilds the city; but alas, with all the old ambiguities of promise and failure, he does so by throwing out foreigners and depopulating the surrounding countryside for the city's advantage. So continues the Jewish history of God's delight and God's pain in the city until in the city of Bethlehem, God's Son is born of Mary.

Jesus and the city

The Galilee of Jesus' day was one of the most densely populated regions of the Roman Empire.[2] Overmann assures us that 'one could not live in any village of lower Galilee and escape the effects and ramifications of urbanization'.[3] This was because the Roman Empire impacted upon the region through their lackeys, the Herods, who sought to replicate the Romans' urban structures of governance across the Galilean region. We recognize this urban influence in the Gospels, where mention is made of urban institutions such as law courts (Matthew 5.25), city market squares (Matthew 23.7), banking (Luke 19.23), absentee landlords (Mark 12.1–12), centurion leaders (Matthew 8.5), urban tax collectors (Matthew 9.10; Luke 5.27), and so on.

At the end of his ministry, Jesus rides into Jerusalem on a donkey, parodying the pomp of the triumphal Roman processions to which the imperial cities were so accustomed. But the city cannot cope with his challenge, so he is arrested, tried and taken outside its walls to be crucified, lest his body should contaminate the purity of the Holy City. According to God's saving plan, Jesus tells his followers to 'stay here in the city until you have been clothed with power from on high' (Luke 24.49, NRSV). As if to right the wrongs of the Tower of Babel, at Pentecost each nationality hears the Good News in its own language and the city of Jerusalem at last becomes a city of 'prayer for all nations', as Isaiah had prophesied. From then on the cities become the launching pads for the missionary outreach of the Church as it takes the Good News of Christ across the global empire.

Starting from Jerusalem, the mission moved from city to city along the road and maritime route-ways which had in earlier times been the military and trade paths along which the Roman Empire had itself expanded its imperial mission. Paul and the Apostles moved from one provincial capital to another, each one standing for a whole region (Antioch for Syria, Philippi for Macedonia, Corinth for Achaia, and so on). A congregation was established in each central city, so that each surrounding region would thereby fall under the influence of the new faith.[4] The Jewish synagogue could not gather unless ten males were present, but Jesus had promised that when only two or three gathered he would be in their midst (Matthew 18.20). So small congregations, some in the richer quarters and others using the workshops of poor four- or five-storey tenement homes, were established in all the major cities.[5] The cities of the Roman Empire were extremely cosmopolitan in style, as analysis of contemporary names and artefacts indicates, and so the missioners had to adopt a radically inclusive strategy and become, as Paul said, 'all things to all people' (1 Corinthians

9.22, NRSV). This caused considerable conflict within the Church, but it was an inclusivity which the new urban environment demanded. So it was that the bishops of the early Church were centred upon and named for the cities, and the *pagani,* or country dwellers, were often the last to be converted – hence 'pagans'.

Our Christian language too was derived from these strong urban influences. The New Testament itself was written in Koine Greek, the trade language of the cities of the Roman world. The word 'liturgy', the biblical word for 'worship', was a term denoting urban philanthropic services, while '*kerygma*', 'the preached message' was originally the herald's worship call to the city. '*Koinonia*' or 'fellowship', referred to the city's many clubs and groups, and '*diakonia*' or 'service' was used in the city for the work of the slaves – hence the term 'deacon'. In each case the common urban language was taken by the early Church, assimilated and transformed, and used in a new exciting way. So it was that the language, structures and mission of the early Church all largely developed within the urban milieu of the Empire.

Throughout the Bible, we see the cities as representing much more than the aggregate of the people within them. They can be addressed in their own right, as if each had a corporate personality. The prophets talk of Nineveh, Babylon and Jerusalem as signs of the cultural values which inhabit them, just as today when we speak of Zurich, Hong Kong, Baghdad, or Washington, each of these city names conjures up a specific picture of values, history and culture.

In the Bible the demanding urban setting is the place where the issues of all society are focused – where the poor suffer, where spiritual battles must be joined, where sin and bloodshed are concentrated and where pride is manifest. Here the 'principalities and powers' can hold sway (Ephesians 6.12). And yet in God's economy there is always hope for the city, even a city as oppressive and cruel as Nineveh. That is why, despite the prophets' obstinacy, Jonah is sent there to proclaim God's promise. God is pained by the city but also delights in her, which moves us to continue the search for urban justice and community despite the enormity of the challenge. 'There is no permanent city for us here; we are looking for the one which is yet to be,' says the writer of the letter to the Hebrews (Hebrews 13.14). So the biblical story concludes with a description of that heavenly city – the 'New Jerusalem', by which all our urban enterprise will be judged.

What is 'urban'?

Before we pass on we must ask to what degree can the cities of antiquity can be said to equate in any way with what we today would call a city. The word 'city' appears no less than 1,200 times in the Bible, but while some cities of Jesus' day, such as Caesarea Maritima, Jerusalem or Tiberias, were certainly extremely large, the 'city' of Capernaum, around which much of Jesus' ministry revolved, hosted only a population of about 1,000, neither could it boast any public buildings that would indicate a civic lifestyle and governance. On the other hand, recent research indicates that cities, towns and villages of that period in Galilee were linked so inseparably that the terms could be used interchangeably in this region which was more urbanized than any other society before the modern era.[6]

But while urban definitions were vague in the biblical period, so are they today. David Clark of Coventry University remarks that while the *United Nations Demographic Yearbook* publishes urban statistics annually, those figures are based upon national definitions of what it is to be urban which are often outdated and subjective.[7] The British government varies its definition to suit the prevailing political climate. Its 1991 Census defined 'urban' as any area with 'land use . . . irreversibly urban in character . . . extending 20 hectares or more and a minimum population of approximately 1,000 persons.' To please the rural lobby, the Urban White Paper in 2000 redefined it to include 'a minimum population of approximately 10,000 persons'.[8] So when the United Nations stated categorically that at the turn of the millennium half the world's population had become 'urban', this was largely a 'guestimate'. We sense that the term is being used so wildly that it has become almost meaningless, and my hope is that during the course of this book the complexities of the urban scene in Britain may become more focused, allowing a more viable vocabulary to emerge.

The Church has tended to assume that the term 'urban theology' has to do only with the poor of the inner cities, even though many urban poor no longer live that close to the city centres, and certainly some urban dwellers are monstrously wealthy! Likewise, it is quite clear that cities are not the only urban areas, and anyone who travels across our landscape will soon be aware of the complexity of the scene, with housing estates, towns and outer-lying suburbs all sprawling across our green and pleasant land. The traveller will also see many a village which looks for all the world stereotypically rural, and yet in my suburban village I doubt if any of its inhabitants could identify the crops in the local fields, whereas the families newly arrived in the heart of the East End from rural Pakistan and Africa would be more likely to know.

As more of the world's population comes to live in cities and towns, so urban influence grows and dominates to such an extent that we no longer have to live in the city to be saturated by its values, its styles and urban imagery. We term this urban domination of our modes of thinking and acting, 'urbanism', and it is so powerfully infectious that it is sometimes difficult for those who are being influenced in this way even to be aware that it is happening to them. We see urban lifestyles being broadcast daily across the globe through advertising, film, communication technology and the mass media, so that 'we are all urban now', and urban manners of thinking and decision-making become the natural default of governments and groups everywhere.

In Jesus' time the powerful influence of the Galilean cities was felt acutely even in the towns and villages. In today's world urbanism's global reach is likewise expanding beyond all expectation to towns and villages around the world. It is difficult to be sure what is truly 'urban' and what is not.

The story of the contemporary city

We have looked at how the Bible tells the urban story and considered some of the issues it raises. We have also realized that our own contemporary urban definitions are somewhat lacking because our contemporary story has become so complex. It will therefore be helpful to see how the disciplines of history and economics have told the story, to see what we can learn from them.

In the 1920s and 1930s the now famous Chicago School of Sociology (among whom we number significant scholars such as Robert Park, Ernest Burgess and Louis Wirth) taught us that cities grow by developing a central core zone or business district, surrounded by concentric zones, each with its own distinct function and supporting role. This was considered to be the inevitable process of urbanization, so the new developing cities of the southern hemisphere were thought to be just beginning that same cyclic process. However, we now realize that things are not that simple.[9] Calcutta is not queuing up to become another Los Angeles – it has its own particular mix of history, geography and culture which is radically different from anything in the Western world, so its story will be its own.

All cities are different, but will nevertheless have some very important things in common. All cities for example bring people together, concentrating and intensifying those problems and issues which are felt less intensely elsewhere. Also, all cities must be open to change and be prepared to respond to new economic and social processes – if not, they die. Similarly, we cannot help but notice how the forces of globalization are imprinting standardization and sameness upon our cities all around the world. Is there a city in the world today where you cannot buy a chilled Coke? But despite all those similarities, alert travellers will still recognize that they are in a different city, with its own history, culture and story. Cities, like human beings, are all different, and one size never fits all.

If the Chicago School's concentric zone theory of urban formation is not the whole story, then neither are theories based solely on economics, because human beings are gregarious, social beings, not merely makers of money. A city therefore needs to develop political, military, religious and social organization if it is to make the most of any economic advantages it may happen to have. The story of the city must therefore be told from many perspectives if it is to be true – economics, history, sociology, geography, theology and politics will all have their place. An informed understanding of the urban will therefore of necessity have to be multi-disciplinary, and this is a salutary warning for the Church which has often sought to engage in urban mission without first discovering this breadth of appreciation.

Despite the great empires of Assyria, Babylonia, Persia and Rome, up to 1550 only 1 per cent of the earth's population was urban. Then, new agricultural, craft and transportation technologies encouraged the accumulation of much greater wealth through trade – the system often referred to as 'mercantilism'. Merchants soon realized that the highest profits were to be made from long-distance trade and so they established large colonial coastal cities through which to funnel wealth to their mother countries. From the eighteenth century on, the new technologies of the industrial revolution sent entrepreneurs and the owners of the new huge mills and factories into overdrive. They required vast quantities of raw materials and expanding markets – two requirements best served by the development of empire – and the cities, already the foci of consumption and trade, now became centres for industrial mass production.

This ruthless entrepreneurialism led in the course of time to the development of prodigious monopolies which, by the end of the nineteenth century, were helping to finance the state-controlled empires within which they functioned. The great military empires of Great Britain and France led the way, closely followed by the United States' emerging empire of economic influence and power. The cities responded to these new concentrations of power by developing even larger industrial plants and expanding their centres to include grandiose financial districts. To house the workers, new estates were built, like Dagenham near the vast Ford Motor Company development, while one of the parishes I served in Birmingham owed its existence to the presence of the tyre factory at Fort Dunlop.

In more recent years monopoly capitalism has developed new global dimensions. New technologies have combined with powerful economic forces to make the world into a 'global village', where the nation states and political alliances are in danger of being eclipsed by the power of the new transnational corporations (TNCs). There were only some 7,000 TNCs in 1969, whereas today there are more than 45,000, dealing mainly in petrol, cars, electronics, food, drugs and chemicals.[10] Suddenly, they control over one-third of all private sector capital, and the turnover of just one TNC often exceeds that of a nation. They have the power to move production around the world to wherever they can find the cheapest labour and raw materials, but retain the real power of management to themselves, normally in the wealthy cities of the northern hemisphere, thereby creating a global division of labour.

The TNCs are also proving to be carriers of the tastes, values and ideologies of Western capitalist culture. For them the bottom line is their place in the global market, so they inculcate a 'commodity' mentality, whereby people and things are evaluated according to how they relate to the market economy. The Silicon Valley companies bring with them a love of high-stake risk-taking, a lack of loyalty to any one employer, and an aversion to working within any strict hierarchy, so when the dot-com business bubble burst, the mentality remained in Silicon Valley that another risk would be worth taking. All these ways of thinking and operating are carried round the world by globalization so that the traveller is assailed by the incongruity of very familiar Western economic landmarks stamped upon the diversity of each local culture. I was stunned to come across a drive-through McDonald's in the middle of the Negev desert, while I hear that the coffee-house chain Starbucks is now a prominent feature of the Forbidden City in Beijing.

However, the brash globalization which seeks to conform us all to Western stereotypes, so that we all end up wearing American baseball caps, also challenges groups to assert themselves and their own cultural values in the face of this pressure. We are seeing the re-emergence of tribalism, nationalism, anti-capitalist ideologies and anti-Western religious radicalism, and the resultant tensions are increasingly being felt in cities and urban centres around the world. The TNCs develop strategies to deal with those localizing trends, altering the specification of their products to suit particular local tastes and preferences around the world. Douglas Daft, the Australian Chairman of Coca-Cola, urged his company, in May 2000, to become 'post-global'. 'During the eighties and well into the nineties, we were riding the wave of globalisation with extraordinary success. But then a very real backlash developed . . . Local governments and individuals responded with a renewed zeal for keeping control over their local politics, local culture and local products.' So Daft's new motto is 'Expanding from global to local'. 'In every country our workforce must truly represent the local society – not because it's politically correct . . . but because the very nature of our business requires that kind of diverse insight and perspective to really flourish.'[11]

The ever-changing city

The radical geographer David Harvey says that capitalism 'builds and rebuilds a geography in its own image',[12] changing towns and cities in accordance with the economic, technological and sociological trends of the time, and with globalization this is happening with unprecedented speed. Cities must respond to this or die. It would seem that this was a lesson which Detroit could not learn. Once the motor car capital of the world, the city came and went in less than a hundred years. Since 1960 Detroit has lost one-third of its population and today nearly every building in its once bustling downtown is abandoned. Cities simply must be responsive to the prevailing forces of history.

The prophet Jeremiah stood in the Temple with a wooden yoke across his shoulders as a symbol of his belief that history is a yoke laid upon the people by their God, and you ignore it at your peril (Jeremiah 28). But Hananiah arrived and broke the prophet's wooden yoke, believing that current historical forces must simply give way to religious ideas and ideologies. He believed that since God had protected the city in the past, so God must do so again, whatever the changing history may indicate. Hananiah's mistake was that he could not comprehend that God may act, in a new historical situation, in altogether new ways, and that the city must therefore change too! Jeremiah understands how much God is concerned for history – for context, for incarnation, for the particular situation – and he therefore returns to the Temple, this time equipped with an unbreakable yoke of iron across his shoulders. History will out! Today, it is particularly in our urban areas that the crucial issues and fresh challenges are most sharply focused. So the urban missioner, more than ever before, must stop using religion as set-piece ideology, like Hananiah, and must reach out to find the theological keys to mission which are appropriate to our new urban challenges. The Greeks used to play a board game called Polis, and *polis* of course is the Greek word for 'city'. Like Jeremiah, they too recognized that the well-being of the city, the *polis*, demands paying attention to the rules of the game, the particular historical circumstances – the new way the pieces are set out on the board each time – and the skills and ingenuity of the many players taking part. New events and unexpected trends demand changes of strategy and a preparedness to jettison old theologies and adopt new mind-sets.

Seeing the big picture

City population figures in the poor regions of the world are reaching unprecedented heights. Pre-industrial rates of fertility, together with post-industrial mortality rates, create steep natural population increments in the cities. Add to this the in-migration from the countryside of those seeking employment and food, and we can see why the population figures go skyrocketing. Already Mexico City, São Paulo and Shanghai are estimated to have populations of over twenty-three million each. In São Paulo, Brazil, a taxi driver told me that during his fifteen years in the job he has been on a constant learning curve because it seemed that every day a new section of the city is built. It is all happening so fast that, world-wide, each year some thirty million people move from the countryside into the cities. That's equivalent to the population of Spain, every year!

There are now fourteen cities with populations over ten million, but by the year 2015 we can expect as many as twenty-seven of that size, with fifteen of them in Asia. Asian countries together already build the equivalent of a city the size of London every six months. By the year 2025, 60 per cent of Africans, 50 per cent of Asians and 85 per cent of Latin Americans will live in urban settlements.[13] Most of those urban in-comers arrive initially in the city centres but gravitate out to the peripheral slums, the *bustees* or *favelas*, which squat on high-risk, hazardous sites without the support of legality, sewerage or infrastructure. For some of the poor it is a self-build first step to home ownership, but for most it is a despairing last step to destitution. As many as 90 per cent of the urban dwellers of Addis Ababa live in slum-shanties, and more than one-third of all the urban dwellers of the developing world have to eke out a life in these abysmal circumstances.[14] The sense of shame one feels as a Westerner visiting these shanties is only eclipsed by the overwhelming hospitality of the people and the resilient laughter of the children. I once stood in such a crowd listening to a politician making false promises to upgrade their hovels, but most of those around me knew only too well that the likelihood of change for the better was minimal. They have, from this grinding daily experience of living against all the odds, so very much to teach the Church about the realities of living by faith, hope and solidarity.

The poor around the world are increasingly aware of the opportunities that exist in a country like ours, and globalization has brought with it an ease of transportation which makes their arrival in Britain more possible by the day. I remember playing with a group of boys who were living in the sewers of Rio de Janeiro. Each year, many of these lads are shot because the shopkeepers believe they intimidate their clientele with their begging. I hoped that one day they would make the journey to the West where their chances of survival and fulfilment are so much greater.

All the changes we have been describing are affecting British towns and cities quite radically day by day. Those who can learn the skills required by the new economy will have bright prospects and an improved standard of living. Those who take on the management, design and research roles in the new economy will reap vast salaries, acquire status and privilege, and a trend-setting lifestyle. New investment capital will transform the look of the city, providing plush office space, waterfront apartments, huge shopping malls and the regeneration of city centres. However, those who are not equipped to take advantage of the system are left to their own devices, with their job security depleted and the safety net of welfare radically diminished. In the UK the poor have become significantly poorer in recent decades, just when an increasingly privatized society is more ready to leave them to it.

*   *   *

In this chapter we have seen how the urban story can be told in many and various ways. The Bible tells of God's pain in the city and how the prophets speak out against its rife injustices. And yet God still calls his people to search, like Abraham, for the city which is yet to be. We have told the urban story from the perspective of other disciplines too, and seen how through the ages cities have changed their shape and structure in order to respond to the economic and social forces of the day. We have mentioned the global processes which are now impacting our urban settlements around the world and changing the direction of the story once again in our own time. The pressures have become so great that it is difficult to believe that our towns and cities can do other than grind to a halt under the stresses and strains of it all. Yet their resilience and dogged stability, in the face of such astounding pressure and lack of sufficient infrastructure, defy belief. What can be the underlying reason for the miracle? Could it be that despite the pain and injustice, God still loves the city? Those who engage in urban mission know what it is to delight with God as they glimpse signs of God's Kingdom day by day among their people. But they also know the despair and the shame as they face the injustice and suffering which are so evident. As Moltmann says, 'God's delight and God's pain. It is out of the tension between these two that hope is born for the Kingdom in which God is wholly in the world and the world is wholly in God.'[15]

3 | The Story of Urban Mission

Our concern for urban ministry and mission is not new, for we follow in the tracks of many who have gone before us, and we do well to learn from the experience and wisdom they have accrued. We have space to mention only a few, so let me focus on some of those people who stand as signposts to the major trends and turning-points of this urban heritage.

*   *   *

Problems for urban mission and ministry go back a long way. It is recorded that Disraeli, in conversation with a bishop who was fearful that the Church was losing the cities, replied, 'Don't be mistaken, my lord, the Church has nothing to lose, for she has never had the city.' Disraeli probably shared with his contemporaries the assumption that urban people were not churchgoers because they were not as moral nor as God-fearing as the rest of the populace. Winnington-Ingram was therefore taken aback on becoming Bishop of London, and wrote, 'My first surprise about east London was its extreme respectability.' Already by then the Anglo-Catholic 'slum-priests' had been serving in the East End for more than thirty years, often joined by members of the newly formed Anglican religious orders. They were driven by a desire to live out an incarnational theology on the margins of society and establishment. Stewart Headlam welded this sacramentalist tradition with the social theology of F. D. Maurice to develop a Christian socialism which continued to inspire towering figures such as St John B. Groser and latterly Kenneth Leech, and is probably the reason why my own left-wing family never quite gave up on me when I became a Christian.

While the Anglo-Catholics were at work in the East End, a great wave of response came from other elements in the Church. The Roman Catholic churches were always full and thriving. The worship was colourful and not book-dependent since the Mass was learnt by heart – and what's more, the priests and nuns came from working-class Irish backgrounds, just like their people. The Free Churches were also deeply involved in the cities. In 1826 David Nasmith founded the Glasgow City Mission, an idea which spawned the London City Mission, which in its heyday boasted no fewer than 500 missionaries deployed across the capital. Founded in 1865, William Booth's Salvation Army offered stirring music and hard-hitting evangelism within a non-denominational framework, later initiating programmes of social care with the establishment of hostels and agricultural colonies. I have a childhood memory of crawling round under the chairs where my great-aunt Ada was attending a meeting at the local 'Sally Army' Citadel in Greenhill Grove. I distinctly remember getting my finger caught in a knot-hole in the floor and have often wondered whether this ranks as my first religious experience!

Universities and public schools established Settlements in the deprived cities which sought, among other things, to act as bridges of goodwill across the class divide. Meanwhile, the 1885 Methodist Conference decided to build Central Missions in the hearts of the cities from which new styles of worship and mission could emanate. Bermondsey Central Hall had boasted a congregation of 1,000 worshippers until September 1939, when one Sunday morning it suddenly fell to 300 and never rose again. Despite this great wave of evangelical response, it never proved possible to resolve the tension between evangelism and social action – a holistic appreciation of mission was yet to be achieved. Neither were they able to cross the class divide – middle-class leadership was still controlling the purse-strings and the policies.

In 1892, across the Atlantic, Dr Graham Taylor set up his 'Chicago Commons' where, with student ordinands, he began to investigate the theological implications of the urban issues which surrounded them – and so what we now call 'urban theology' at last began in earnest. It was to prove a model for much that would follow both in the UK and USA, as I myself learnt when in 1968 I enrolled on a Chicago-inspired programme run by G. Bill Webber, the chief pastor of the East Harlem Protestant Parish. The style was one of hands-on engagement, learning both from the inner-city inhabitants of New York City and engaging in seminars with the urban theologians of Union Seminary.

It was the First World War which highlighted the inadequacies of theological training in the UK. Chaplains returned from the harsh realities of life and death in the trenches knowing that a radical rethink was necessary. So it was decided to convert an old prison at Knutsford to become a new kind of theological college where young men could train for ordination in a new way.[1] The college later moved to Brasted and then became the Aston Training Scheme which carried on the brave tradition until the Church of England withdrew funding. In addition to this training initiative, army chaplains were commissioned to minister in the munitions factories. My grandmother was working on the production line at Woolwich Arsenal and was surprised to experience a visit from a chaplain. But in this way industrial chaplaincy was born, and soon became an established part of the post-war ministerial provision of the Church, supported by the theological work of the Industrial Christian Fellowship and the William Temple College. William Temple had been the first president of the Workers' Educational Association and an inspiring founder chairman of COPEC, the National Conference on Politics, Economics and Citizenship. In 1941, the year he became Archbishop of Canterbury, Temple published his short book *Christianity and Social Order*. In it he set out what has been called the theory of 'middle axioms'. 'The Church must announce Christian principles . . . then pass on to Christian citizens, acting in their civic capacity, the task of re-shaping the existing order in closer conformity to the principles . . . The Church may tell the politician what ends the social order should promote; but it must leave to the politician the devising of the precise means to those ends.' This became the official line of the Church for many years, but was always a bone of contention for those engaged in urban ministry.

The William Temple College helped the industrial chaplains to find their feet but in 1957 one of the most influential books on the life of faith and the world of work was written by Ted Wickham, then Sheffield Cathedral's Industrial Missioner. In *Church and People in an Industrial City* he argued that the old parish system had failed to address secular industrial Britain. The only hope was the industrial chaplaincy system. I was very taken by the vision myself and in 1963 was on the verge of buying my first pair of steel-capped boots to take my place in the steel furnaces of Scunthorpe, but I bottled out and went off to Birmingham instead to become a folk singer. That was the year when John Robinson, Bishop of Woolwich, published *Honest to God* in which he sought to be 'utterly honest about the terms in which the Faith can be truthfully presented today'. Its intellectual honesty seemed quite revolutionary for a conventional Church. Those who followed in Ted Wickham's train largely accepted the secular optimism of the age, and in 1965 the Harvard Professor of Divinity, Harvey Cox, enlivened us all with his book *The Secular City*, in which he described the city as an exciting symbol of the soon-to-be realized Kingdom of God.

Although civil riots had occurred less than two years before in Birmingham, Alabama, Cox nevertheless was a voice which at last refused to adopt theology's usual anti-urban bias. He obviously did not convince Jacques Ellul who soon after remarked in his *Meaning of the City*, 'like a vampire . . . the city devours men . . . the essential goal of the cities – to make every man captive'. Ellul's famous book certainly depressed me!

Meanwhile an alternative style of British urban theology had been encouraged by the slightly earlier work of the Parish and People Movement which sought to place the Parish Communion at the heart of British church life. A sacramental awareness of the Church as the Body of Christ in the world was celebrated each Sunday around the altar and books such as *The Parish in Action* by the Bishop of Stepney, Joost de Blank, helped to redress the complaint of Industrial Mission that the parish churches had separated themselves from the urban people of Britain. Having grown up in a 'Parish and People' parish I well remember the excitement at the revolutionary incarnational theology that was being preached Sunday by Sunday and being worked out daily in the lives of the working-class congregation. Ernie Southcott, a leading light of the movement, came one Sunday. I recall his enormous hands flapping so violently to emphasize his point that we all thought that Ernie and the pulpit would soon take off. Stephen Verney, then a Canon at Coventry Cathedral, was another animated preacher. He was responsible for bringing together people from thirty-three nations to a conference called 'People and Cities' in order, as he put it, 'to search for a positive vision of the city of the future'.[2] What was to prove truly prophetic about his work was that he realized that any urban theology worth its salt had to take account of both the international context and of what the disciplines of urban studies had to teach us. It was to be a long time before urban missioners really learnt those lessons.

The new urban theological practitioners

The 1970s saw a growing disillusionment with the modernist optimism of the 1960s. The concrete high-rise flats were crumbling, the Church looked very old-fashioned, and industrial mission had seemed to come adrift from its Christian roots. In 1969, the Methodist radical John Vincent returned from visiting lectureships in the USA to establish the Urban Theology Unit (UTU) in Sheffield along with a group of committed Christian friends and activists determined to reflect theologically upon the current urban scene. Vincent's vision of 'doing urban theology' was in the tradition of Graham

Taylor in Chicago and Webber in New York, but also inherited something of the European biblical scholarship tradition in which Vincent himself had been schooled. This radical endeavour attracted many enquirers, and soon a resident community of theological action and reflection formed the base for a national and international network of urban theologians inspired by the charismatic and decidedly challenging leadership of John Vincent.

This new spirit was inspiring others too, for simultaneously Donald Reeves and Tony Dyson teamed up to create the Urban Ministry Project. UMP was designed to introduce ordinands to the harsh realities of city living and to encourage them to reflect theologically and prayerfully upon urban issues. The Project became famous for 'the Plunge' which challenged each participant to spend four nights on the streets at the mercy of the city night-life. A little earlier, in the same spirit, a group of evangelical Christians, including David Sheppard, Ted Roberts, Frank Deeks and John Hunter, had met together to bemoan the gulf that still existed between the British working-class and the Church, and set about the formation of what was to become the Evangelical Urban Training Project – EUTP. Soon joined by the wonderfully ebullient Neville Black, and the new Rector of St Martin's, Birmingham, Peter Hall, the EUTP was to be an inspiration to the evangelical wing of the Church to find again its commitment to urban mission and help train men and women for the work. Neville Black set up from his Anglican parish in his beloved Liverpool a radically alternative form of training for Christian urban leadership. GUML (the Group for Urban Ministry and Leadership) used many of the same theological tools as Vincent's UTU, but this time it was specifically geared to bringing indigenous working-class people into authorized leadership in the parishes. John and Neville between them proved to be a strong and challenging voice to the Church. When Neville finished his time as EUTP Project Officer, his place was taken by Jim Hart who had worked with him to produce an inspiring programme called 'Learning Without Books'. It was especially designed to facilitate those who, as it explained, 'can read but don't'.

In September 1974 a meeting at St Deiniol's Library, Hawarden, brought all these inspiring leaders of the movement together and, as John Hunter relates, 'it was the occasion when many of the people engaged in Urban Mission had gathered for the first time. There were those who came to look back to Hawarden as a birth date for Urban Mission concerns in the UK.' Many of those attending met again later at Windsor, along with other important leaders such as Jim Punton from Frontier Youth Trust and Michael Eastman from Scripture Union, and resolved to unite the liberal and evangelical leaders in what became the Urban Mission Training

Association, where we could share good practice and do our urban theology together. We became very excited in those meetings by the writings of Paulo Freire,[3] and Ian Fraser, a passionate Scot and member of the Iona Community, brought to our attention ways of doing theology which were being developed in Latin America, where Freire had originated. As with our own style it began from ordinary people's own experiences and their own reflections upon them. CAFOD (the Catholic Fund for Overseas Development), along with Maggie Pickup, the Catholic Director of the Saltley Trust in Birmingham, invited three of the best Brazilian exponents of the method, José Marins, Teo Trevisan and Carolee Chanona,[4] to visit Britain on an annual basis to train many of us in this exciting methodology, which drew heavily upon the insights of Liberation Theology. I had already set up in inner-city Birmingham a group of working-class lay Christians who, using this method, found themselves creating from their own urban experience a vibrant theology of domination and freedom. They started from their own God-given experience of life and interpreted that in the light of the Christian traditions so that it became a springboard for committed action in the community. I told the whole story in *Power to the Powerless*, and at the book launch the publisher was somewhat taken aback when the group themselves took over, providing for everyone a wonderful meal of curried goat and rice. Sue Draper, one of the group, gave a short speech. 'Until I joined this group,' she said, 'I thought that incarnation was something that came out of a tin!'

One of the ways in which the new urban scene of the 1970s brought us face to face with different experiences was through the growing involvement in theology and ministry of black and Asian Christians. The Black and White Partnership at Selly Oak, Birmingham, enabled Christians from every type of congregational style to share in depth something of their life journey and understanding of God. Barney Pityana brought a black intellectual rigour to the conversations while David Horn and John Wilkinson taught us all a great deal from their experience of listening to the black congregations with whom they worked. Barry Thorley, a vicar in Handsworth, and Wilfred Wood, later Bishop of Croydon, were able to speak from a deep personal experience of being black in the British Church. Rajinder Daniel spoke from the Asian experience and the Ashram Acres community in Sparkbrook, Birmingham, brought Asian Muslims and black and white Christians together around a common cause and employment project.

Despite all the excitement of these projects and others like them around the country, urban theology and mission were still not acknowledged by the mainstream churches to be of critical importance to Christian life in the UK. They were still not taken very seriously in the theological colleges nor in the ongoing life of the mainstream denominations. We had the feeling that urban mission and theology were considered to be a minority interest for 'those who liked that sort of thing'. The class bias of Anglican ministry was little understood, even though Eric James was forever accusing some of the inner-city vicarages of being middle-class oases. On many occasions, black Christians had been turned away at church doors and politely asked to worship elsewhere, while rarely was any investment made to enable the congregations of inner-city churches to embolden their mission. In 1974, a decisive attempt was therefore made by Bishop David Sheppard to bring the excitement and challenge of ministry in poor urban areas to the attention of the Church at large. Many readers recognized in his optimistic evangelical book, *Built as a City*, a description of the Church as they understood it. The book was a *tour de force*, setting out in 300 riveting pages his description of the needs and promise of the inner city, then followed by 300 more pages on how the Church should respond, actively and theologically. *Built as a City* proved to be a prophetic invitation to a conservative Church to wake up to the fact that something should and could be done, and in 1985 the Church of England responded to that prophetic invitation by producing a report which was to change things profoundly.

Faith in the City

In 1981, Lord Scarman produced a report on the horrific riots that had taken place in Brixton, soon followed by others in Birmingham, Tottenham and Bristol. In response, Archbishop Robert Runcie spoke out. He said, 'There are, of course, temptations to withdraw from the inner cities' and then promised, 'as far as I have any influence, I am determined that we should maintain our presence in the most sensitive areas and allocate our resources accordingly.' Within a year his Commission, whose membership included David Sheppard, had been set up and began its two-year investigation, finally issuing its report, *Faith in the City*, in December 1985. The press had a field day!

The Times carried as its main headline, 'Church and State launched into new public quarrel'. It is hard for us today to comprehend the anger of the Thatcher government on seeing the Church of England raise the curtain on the reality of the inner cities and outer estates of Britain. Paul Johnson, fearing that left-wing activists had infiltrated the established Church, wrote the next day in the *Daily Mail*, calling the report 'a flawed gospel that is beneath contempt'. Strangely, however, no one ever contradicted any of the statistics or findings of the Report since they were taken from the government's own data. Malcolm Grundy insightfully commented how this furore 'showed what confusion can be caused within the ranks of the establishment, let alone with the public, when a national institution like the Church of England publishes a report which brings into the open the problems of a particular section of English society who do not have a voice of their own – except on occasion to riot in the streets'.[5]

The Report was divided into three sections. The first amassed data describing the economic decline and social decay of what it termed the 'Urban Priority Areas'. The second section challenged the Church to respond, and the third addressed the nation with a series of recommendations. It recommended the setting up by the Church of a fund to finance urban missional activities and projects, the Church Urban Fund, and asked the whole Church and nation to attend immediately to urban issues as a priority. At last, the wheel had turned in our favour.

We saw a pouring out of publications about city mission, and many colleges, realizing that they were placed in largely rural settings, established inner-city projects where ordinands could stay and learn from local pastors and practitioners. More priests began to find the idea of urban ministry attractive and urban parishes were no longer the Cinderellas on the vacancies list. When at last money became available from the Church Urban Fund to kick-start projects and programmes and employ urban church workers, many church buildings were transformed and new resources given to congregations who had before been struggling on, unnoticed.

One criticism of *Faith in the City* was first raised by Frank Field, MP. He wrote,

> While the report is a first-class piece of work . . . it could have been produced by any group of decent minded individuals. What should have made it special and different from secular efforts was its theology – of God's vision of the world, the nature of man [*sic*] and his part in working out this design. Instead of this starting point, the theological analysis is tacked on to the end.

In fact the whole of the third chapter of the Report was devoted to theology, but Field was right to say that it did not appear to be a major building block of the Commission's work. It adopted the 'Middle Axiom' approach earlier favoured by William Temple and tended to be conservative in its theological stance, contending that, 'Whatever the implications for society as a whole (and these indeed have been profound) the characteristic sphere of Jesus' ministry was that of personal relationships and individual responses.' Others therefore set about producing theological contributions to the debate, but most seemed somewhat academic and unrelated to the urban world we knew. Nicholas Bradbury produced a valuable book, *City of God?*, which was packed with insights into urban ministry deriving from a more pastoral perspective, while *Inner City God*, an earlier study by Geoffrey Ahern and Grace Davie, looked at the religiosity of the working-class urban people as expressed in folk religion.

Nevertheless, despite years of work on the part of urban theologians prior to the *Faith in the City* report and beyond it, the British Church at large still seemed unable to integrate practical urban action with theological reflection. The Methodist Church had been running its *Mission Alongside the Poor* programme, in parallel with *Faith in the City*, which promised well, as did the creative work of Colin Marchant, Terry Drummond and others, but the insights of these endeavours were not as widely taken up as they deserved. The Church Urban Fund had enabled a vast number of urban projects to develop, buildings to be built or re-structured, and personnel to be employed, but as if to mirror the inadequacy of *Faith in the City*'s own theology, rarely if ever was in-built theological reflection among the criteria for CUF funding. In 1997 Ann Morisy's *Beyond the Good Samaritan* gently but firmly pleaded that while programmes of care for the community's welfare were excellent, things could really lift off if a note of critical theological reflection could be introduced.

During this intervening period tremendous expertise was nevertheless built up by the British Church in the field of community development,[6] both at a professional level by such groups as the Churches Community Work Alliance, and by congregations which utilized the Parish Audit programme which had been recommended in the Report. The Audit asked each congregation to scrutinize its context and respond carefully in order that it should become more true to the Report's criteria for good practice – that each church should be 'local, outward-looking, participative and ecumenical'.[7] In time, rarely was there an urban church without a project, but rarely was the project fully integrated into the prayer life, the worship and the theological reflection of the congregation.

The American connection

In telling this story of urban mission, ministry and theology in the UK, we must not forget that throughout this period a great deal of mutual learning was going on across the Atlantic between the UK and the USA. Even as early as 1964 the Episcopal Church in the USA had set up an urban fund to support experimental urban ministries, as well as a new publication, *Church in Metropolis*. In 1976, an Urban Bishops' Coalition was set up, prefiguring our Urban Bishops' Panel, which programmed a series of seven 'urban hearings' out of which grew the Episcopal Urban Caucus (EUC). It was the telling of that story in *To Hear and to Heed* that led to our own UK Urban Hearings some years later. Raymond Bakke's visits to the UK resulted in Jim Hart editing his papers to produce *The Urban Christian*, which was to prove a great boost to the confidence of our urban theologians of a more evangelical frame of mind. Bakke had years of experience as a Baptist minister in the inner city of Chicago and then, as a teacher, had travelled the cities of the world bringing a welcome global perspective to his teaching. Harvie Conn, a large, brave, bearded evangelical, did much of his important biblical urban studies in concert with Manuel Ortiz, who both befriended the British urban scene to our advantage – Manuel, along with Eldin Villafañe, brought us a deep understanding of ethnicity and culture. Jim Wallis from Washington became a good friend to many of us and shared insights into how our Christian faith must radicalize our political activism. When I myself lived in the States in the late 1960s, I had been introduced to a radical political programme of Community Organizing based upon the Machiavellian philosophy of Saul Alinsky, and Community Organizing has more recently been taken up in parts of the UK and, over the years, transformed into a more theologically sound enterprise. So, this mutual relationship with the USA has continued through the years and has recently been offering us new perspectives on urbanology and theological studies much to our advantage – which we will be discussing in later chapters.

Learning from our mission story

It is certainly fair to conclude that a great deal has been accomplished across Britain in the course of our long engagement with urban mission. Churches have established a good track record of long-term commitment to urban communities. Government programmes and initiatives have come and gone, but the urban parish churches have stayed, and while others begin to talk of 'capacity building' as if it were a new thing, the churches have been building up the abilities and skills of their local members for generations. Many Christians have played very significant roles indeed in the formal and informal networks of the community. As well as investing in people, the Church has also provided significant urban community halls and churches, which have offered, through God's grace, meeting places of sanctuary and solace as well as opportunities for worship, growth and celebration. We have learnt from our clergy that living in the community with your family is the only way to prove your commitment, gain the trust of your community and learn from it. It has often been the case that the local congregation continues to be small and comparatively unprofessional – but in that very way it has proved how representative of the community it actually is. The Church has, time and again, been called upon to act as the bridge-builder between conflicting local groups and people, and although so often it is taken for granted or ignored as irrelevant, it has turned out to be a life-saver of those whom society has disregarded or given up on.

But there are also unresolved issues. First, there are questions of power. Fr Austin Smith, prayerfully reflecting from his basement flat in Liverpool 8, asks questions about the frenetic rush to activity and project work on the part of the Church. He concludes that many of our projects and government partnerships have been power-grabbing, and have kept control firmly out of the hands of those whom Christ wanted to empower. Austin wrote,

> The fundamental problem of community power in the midst of Innercityism is its lack of access to political, economic and cultural resources. This is not to suggest that we can dispense with community action and community work, but it is to suggest that those of us who are so-called 'professionals' must accept the fact that we cannot be partners to or with community action without simultaneously accepting and identifying the dimension of change which must take place in the sphere of the political, economic and cultural holders, not to say manipulators, of those resources. In other words, at the very heart of the exercise there is a demand for a radical transference of power. This is a radical problem, not only for the State, but it is also a radical problem of understanding and perception for the ministry of the Church.[8]

There have also been from time to time power struggles between urban mission styles. Engagement and commitment to urban mission on the part of the evangelical community have become over the years both widespread and often qualitative. But the unfortunate spin-off of this development has been the demise of the urban mission alliance that had been carefully nurtured between the evangelicals and the more liberal urban theologians – and the liberals eventually got to the point where they felt that the evangelicals were stealing the show. National urban mission conferences seemed to be dominated by the one constituency – and no doubt, at times, evangelicals felt it was the other way about.

There remains also the power question of leadership – some arguing that only those who are really locally born and bred should lead urban mission, others feeling at liberty to parachute in and exit out, as other professionals are apt to do. This raises up the issues of race, gender and class, which often cause our church leaders to misunderstand, patronize or disempower those who are 'led'.

After the question of power, the next unresolved issue seems to revolve around differing understandings of the nature of our mission. If our mission is to proclaim the Good News, the question then arises, what the Good News – the gospel – may possibly be for the people of the city. It was an issue which threatened to tear the Salvation Army apart when it moved into its hostel care work, leaving to its Citadels the work of direct evangelism. Some argued that the Good News was evangelism, others to feed and clothe the hungry. Some hold that working for structural justice is not part of mission, or even if it is, then it is only brought about by personal conversion. There are those who believe too that we proclaim a gospel that is already there with the people, while others maintain we are there to bring it to them.

Another difficulty stems from the word 'urban' itself. Nearly all the models of urban mission that were developed during these years assumed that the focus for urban mission is the poor and needy of the inner-city areas. There was little appreciation of the subtle but very real relationships that exist between various parts of each city, the rich and the poor, the city centre and the outer estates, suburbs, towns and villages. The lack of a holistic perspective has left our urban mission wanting.

The final unresolved issue relates to the question of 'praxis', but let me say immediately that by this word I do not mean 'practice' but something much more dynamic than that. Some books on urban theology give the impression that the writers have never ventured on to the streets of a city or estate for years. Other books describe the story of a project, but never compare or contrast it with the Jesus story. There is no evidence of an integration of theory and practice, of reflection and action, and it is this integration which we refer to as 'praxis'. Contextual theology at its best seeks to be rounded in its praxis, but many theological teachers and trainers still only understand 'contextual theology' to mean theology which is *abstracted* from a particular context. The seminal work of the Belgian priest, Joseph Cardijn, in the 1920s, gave us many tools for 'doing theology' in a thoroughly integrated and praxis-centred manner, but old bad habits die hard. This was why I wrote *Let's Do Theology* in 1990, in order to describe this more ambitious way of doing theology as a democratic and dynamic interplay of Christian action and theological reflection. In that book I describe how the praxis of theology begins with telling the story, after which we move on to a more thorough analysis of the issue at hand. In just this way, having now told the urban mission story, we can move on to the second part of this book – an analysis of today's urban scene.

Part 2

The Urban Challenge Today

An analysis of our present predicament and its significance for us

4 | The New Urban Challenge

The Church has always believed that telling the Christian story is essential – but more than that, it has sought to become part of that Christian story – to be and do the things which that story demands. So the great traditions of our faith are rehearsed and celebrated by the Church, but then comes the challenge of how we, in our generation, should live out that story and be true to that story in our new situation. To do that well, the Church has a duty to be critically alert to what the 'new situation' may be.

In the first part of this book we have been telling the urban story – from the biblical perspective, from the point of view of the urban disciplines and the different schools of urban studies, and latterly we have been telling the story of the British Church's response. The task in this second section of the book is to see if the urban scene has been moving on apace for this new generation. And I have to say immediately that my sense is that the city and the wider urban scene, although much the same in so many ways, is already a different place for my children than it has been for me. Their urban experience is more cosmopolitan, more international, more dependent upon new technologies, more consumer-centred, more privatized, more ethnically aware, more noisy, polarized, polluted and more designer-orientated than my urban experience has been. The changes in just these last ten years would have taken generations to achieve in former times, but I sense that our theology, our mission practices and our ways of being Church are still more attuned to the needs of a past generation than they are to the one which is emerging.

A new urban scene

If we cast our minds back to the years immediately following the publication of the *Faith in the City* report, we will soon be aware that since then there has been a whole raft of changes. In 1985 when the Report was published, the Cold War still divided East from West, and the electronic technology, which has transformed our everyday lives and the physical environment in which we work, was still in its infancy. The words 'globalization' and 'branding' had not yet registered in the public consciousness, and the financial market had yet to be deregulated, which was in turn to transform the very nature and meaning of trade. We were not aware of how the great mega-cities of the southern hemisphere were beginning to impact our lives, nor how our new place in Europe was to introduce a move to regional government on the European model. We could see that British industries were being affected by new international economic pressures, but we did not foresee how much our coal, steel, automobile and agricultural communities were going to be ravaged or transformed. We could not have predicted that in 1998 Microsoft would take over from the production giant General Electric as the world's biggest company. The inner cores of our old cities were already suffering, being denuded of their industry and population, but who could have guessed that Canning Town, the old slum district where my parents grew up, would be gentrified to the extent that it is now too expensive for me to rent a room there?

During this intervening period many of the cities of northern England have suffered depopulation at the expense of an overheated south-east, which in turn struggles to cope with its resultant overcrowding and affluence. The national inequality of income and wealth has increased rather than reduced, so that between 1988 and 1999 the top 1 per cent of our population increased their share of the country's wealth from 17 per cent to 23 per cent. Migration patterns have changed the colour and culture of many of our cities and towns, so that there are now more Muslims in the UK than Methodists and Baptists put together. Black and Asian Christians who have arrived since 1985 have been received by the churches in a very different way from their predecessors, I'm glad to say, and that in turn has radically changed the face of our multi-ethnic congregations. Cultural diversity creates a new cosmopolitan urban atmosphere, and this, along with leisure and fun in the towns and cities, increasingly attracts the young.

Since 1985, regeneration, partnership and sustainable communities have become the political buzz-words. An Urban White Paper, the first to address the urban situation in such a focused way since 1976, has been agreed by Parliament, and urban parishes have been overrun and often overwhelmed by government schemes and initiatives. The new partnership ethos of regeneration goes hand in hand with a burgeoning of the voluntary sector in an increasingly privatized social care system which now expects voluntary and community groups to see themselves merely as service providers for governments. Urban renewal programmes have demolished and rebuilt housing estates. Private sector investment has turned old wharves and docklands into fashionable new leisure centres, and urban sprawl is eating away at the countryside. Market-led change has created shopping malls which stand as the new cathedrals of consumerism, and new office buildings, hotels and colleges tower into the air. The very face of our cities and towns has been changed, and all this in just a few years.

Urban ministers are seeing too the increasing use of alcohol and drugs as an escape from the deprivation of poor areas, while affluent youngsters accustom themselves to a designer drug culture and social life. Americans now spend as much each year on illegal drugs as they do on soft drinks ($57 billion) and our drugs trade is globally linked to theirs, so our future looks bleak. Drug cartels contribute to the escalating gun crime and an ever-increasing fear of violence on the streets. In consequence, many now gate and defend their homes, and again we look with dismay to see that in Florida the city of Atlantis is currently spending 70 per cent of its annual budget on guards and gates. Ninety million Americans live in gated enclosures, and the trend has caught on in Britain. And as if all this change were not enough, the terrorist destruction of the World Trade Center on 11 September 2001 has made our world yet more fragile. To the ordinary urban person, things feel different from 1985 and *Faith in the City*, when so many of our urban mission strategies were formulated.

Over recent years, urban studies has become, as never before, a major discipline in our universities and urban institutes. What is more, a significant number of these specialists are keen to share their learning and expertise with those of us who have hands-on responsibility for the urban scene. A great deal of this academic learning has been introduced to the Churches through the work of Andrew Davey,[1] and the Open University has produced a very fine collection of publications in its *Understanding Cities* series. The new urbanologists are teaching us that, whereas in the past we had been inclined to see the city first as a mechanism, and then as an organism with each part functioning in balance with the next, this 'big picture' will no longer do. They see the city as a contested space with many individuals and groups all fighting their corner. Doreen Massey, one of the leading British scholars, talks of the 'mixity' of cities and urban places.

A second major thrust of this academic study centres around the all-important issue of power. The title of a short book by three British geographers says it all – *Cities for the Many Not the Few*. It stakes out 'an alternative vision for urban life centred around the energies of its inhabitants and geared towards meeting social needs and developing capabilities . . . in ways in which living together in cities is an enriching and creative experience'.[2] This sort of practical interest puts their learning at our disposal in a very refreshing and useful way, especially when at the heart of their message is their wish to democratize our towns and cities.

Leonie Sandercock, an Australian professor of planning, is one such, who objects to the way in which planners and architects have moved in on locations without a thought for those who live there. She points out that they have planned and built without recognizing that in doing so they mark a community with their own political assumptions and social values. She says that the people who know better than the planners what the values of that community are, and what that community 'means', are the local people themselves. Neighbourhoods are all about community relationships, but you can destroy those relationships very easily and at ruinous cost because their quality is what counts for a 'good' city, or a 'good' town. Sandercock helps us to do a power analysis of urban life to see how easy it is to throw power around and ruin our treasured urban communities. That's why Keith Proctor in Britain has set up, with the Churches National Housing Coalition, a project to help people from local communities to take the lead themselves in the regeneration of their housing estates. His *Community Led Estate Regeneration Handbook* is a collection of stories, told by the residents themselves, of how they took the lead in employing their own architects so that community relationships were strengthened and not destroyed.

Other urbanologists have majored on how cities around the world are linked today into a global framework, so that we cannot understand what makes one tick without appreciating its relationship to the next. Saskia Sassen, another important name on the scene, has argued that according to the intensity of the economic transactions between them, the great cities form up in a sort of hierarchy, the prime centres being New York, London, Tokyo, Hong Kong and so on. These are the 'Global Cities' which have very intimate connections one with another, controlling between them the major financial transactions of the world. Then come the 'World Cities' which have tremendous power and prestige but not the same degree of financial clout and connectivity. Many of the new megacities of the developing world come into this category. Then will come the 'Core Cities', or second-level cities, like Birmingham, Newcastle, Sheffield, Manchester or Bristol. Between them the core cities house 30 per cent of England's population and should become the core economic engines of growth for their surrounding regions. Sassen points out, however, that there will be many cities, particularly in Africa, which have no place in the urban hierarchy because they are increasingly peripheral to the great axes of economic power, and she sees no future for them. So begin the great migrations of population seeking to escape to the cities of greater power and economic promise, and this creates increasing congestion in the more wealthy cities of the world, with all the conflict and tension that produces.

Seeing all this happening around us has led some academics like David Harvey to question the processes that are leading to such disparity and suffering. He begins to question the politics and morality on which it is all happening. He looks for other value systems and accuses the world of drifting back to the old imperialisms of the past. If we are going to have urban lives that are worth living, he suggests, then we need to refashion our dreams and find more democratic ways to fulfil them. It soon becomes clear, reading the books and papers of these modern urbanologists like Harvey, that in order to understand the dynamics driving these urban changes we must address what has become known as 'globalization'. So let us now turn our minds in that direction.

Globalization

Globalization is not a new phenomenon. At its height the British Empire alone boasted 390 million people through its colonization of some fifty-two nations, all interlocking across the globe. As a child, I remember being told by the teacher that more than one-third of the world's land surface, which was coloured pink on the globe, 'belongs to us'. Jesus himself knew what it was like to live in a world dominated by 'global' interests. The Roman imperial network facilitated trade and travel from India to Britain, and throughout that world Koine Greek would have been the common trading language. Farming had, by the time of Christ, been overwhelmed by Roman agri-business, turning Galilean farmers off their land and making them into day labourers. The fishing towns of the Sea of Galilee were now dominated by the new city of Tiberias and the fish-salting factories of Magdala, all linking the prodigious food production of Galilee with the breadth of the Empire. We will look more carefully at the biblical period later, but suffice it here to say that Jesus knew what imperial globalization felt like. He would also have recognized that globalization was then, as it is now, largely processed through its cities.

There are three factors which work together to generate our modern globalization. They are technology, politics and economics. We'll consider each in turn.

1. Technology

In 1837 the telegraph was invented, at last solving the problem of distance in human communication. Ten years earlier, the first steamship crossed the Atlantic, and in 1927 Lindbergh flew non-stop over it – the great ocean had become 'the Pond'. Fibre optics and the World Wide Web were developed in the 1980s, but even by 1993, the year Bill Clinton arrived in the White House, there were still only fifty websites. Now it is estimated that there are 400 million sites and the figure is forever rising. Communications technology allows capital and information to speed around the globe, but also facilitates the migration of colossal numbers of human beings so that in almost every city we can expect to be confronted by different cultures, different languages and different religions. There are now more than a million Japanese living in São Paulo and more Salvadoreans in Los Angeles than live in San Salvador.

2. Politics

In 1989 the Berlin Wall fell and Europe was no longer divided between East and West, opening up Eastern markets as never before. A good friend of mine, working for Western military intelligence, said to me that with the Soviet Union gone, 'we'll just have to find a new enemy if we're going to hold together'. They proved to be prophetic words. Once the 'second world' was no more, the 'first' and the 'third' worlds found themselves meeting even more on the streets of the cosmopolitan cities as the first world ratcheted up its influence and presence across the globe.

The political influence of the 'first world' is epitomized in the alliance which was formed between Margaret Thatcher, Helmut Kohl and Ronald Reagan. In their minds, no longer did politics have a welfare orientation, but the function of government became more concerned with enticing private investment to fund its operations. Labour rights were reduced to a whisker, and everything and everyone was exposed to the forces of the market. This allowed Thatcher to issue her battle-cry, 'TINA – There Is No Alternative' – to market forces.

These political changes went hand in hand with the prodigious technological advances that were being made – but neither would have been able to function without the third motor or generator of globalization playing its part, and that motor was economics.

3. Economics

Money has been at the heart of 'globalization' – the word itself first appearing in the 1970s' advertisements for American Express credit cards.

It was then used in the financial press to bolster arguments for deregulation, before moving into the popular vocabulary. The London stock market was developed in the eighteenth century, but it took until 27 October 1987 for the London Stock Exchange to be de-regulated, after the American example. It then became possible to trade much more freely. This was the so-called 'Big Bang', and when coupled with the newly available technology, it sent the markets into overdrive – 'turbo-capitalism' had now arrived. In milliseconds, investment capital could now chase cheap raw materials and labour markets around the globe, investing and de-investing at the wink of an eye. In 1970, well before the Big Bang, 90 per cent of international trade transactions around the world were in the form of industrial capital – what we may generally think of as 'real things'. The remaining 10 per cent of transactions was in the more abstract area of 'finance'. By the year 2000, the whole thing had reversed. Now, despite the massive overall increase in international transactions, as much as 90 per cent of those transactions are in abstract finance. It really has all become so abstract that when anti-globalization protesters attack firms like Nike and McDonald's they are in fact only addressing 10 per cent of the problem. Every day one and a half trillion dollars-worth of business is traded on the currency markets, and just four days of this trade is equivalent to the total world trade in goods and services for a whole year. Of that great total, 95 per cent is purely speculative – treating money as a commodity in its own right.[3] The whole system is quite vulnerable, however, as we saw when the bubble burst in Thailand and the greed of the financiers nearly brought the whole edifice crashing down. When the scandalous financial dealings of Enron and Andersens in Houston were exposed, the repercussions were felt around the globe. As house prices rocketed and pensions plummeted there was not a suburban street in the UK that was not affected.

Globalization, with its three motors of technology, politics and economics, may sound very abstract. However, in order for this dynamic to function well, it has to have the necessary 'hardware' of people, locations and machinery, and that is why cities are so crucial to the global picture. The cities offer the necessary concentration of infrastructure, personnel, know-how and personal interface, for the three generators of globalization to come together and resource one another.

The industrial cities were originally necessary in order to allow industry to concentrate all its means of production in one location. Today, however, raw materials can be gathered in one continent, the parts made in another and the product assembled in a third. Hornby is still a British company, but its train-sets are made in China. So it is that productive industry moves out to other locations, but the cities still thrive for other reasons. First, they offer the close proximity, personal services, security systems, child care, food and entertainment that the well-paid workers of the global system look for. Second, ideas, capital, commodities and support services are interwoven in the cities, which can then become the command centres of global capitalism – each one linked to other cities across the globe, with headquarters of transnational corporations and finance, legal and design services clustering like bees around a honey pot. Third, although Western cities are no longer the key manufacturing centres, they are the consumer demand centres which provide the vast markets which the system requires. For all these reasons, the cities remain as the crucial linchpins of the global system.[4]

This globalization has created remarkable benefits for our society. We all recognize that there have been exceptional advances in scientific discovery, leading to the virtual eradication in the developed world of many diseases and an increase in our life expectancy. There has been an explosion in the spread and ready availability of information and knowledge. With this sharing has come the expectation of choice, and more people now live democratically under chosen governments than ever before. People across the world know more about good governance, environmental justice and human rights. Millions have been lifted out of poverty and many have experienced observable wealth increases. Our cities have become exciting international places offering us a wonderful kaleidoscope of cultures. But having said all this, we also have to recognize that this is only one half of the globalization story.

On 11 July 2000, in Payatas in the city of Manila, a rubbish dump collapsed in the middle of the night. Homes that had perched upon that dump just vanished and 218 people immediately perished. Three hundred more were lost for ever somewhere under the rubbish – lost under the trash of the global city. This disaster was typical of the daily plight of the global urban poor who find themselves, in varying degrees, at the mercy of pollution, others' over-consumption, the breakdown of urban infrastructure, the lack of tenure rights, exclusion from the benefits of the market, spatial segregation, poor health services, disease-ridden water and, above all, sheer poverty. The list seems endless – and all this while living within sight of flaunted affluence and power.

That great symbol of globalization, the World Wide Web, is indicative of the hidden downside of the whole complex structure. The name itself gives a very misleading picture when we know that 80 per cent of the world's population has never made a phone call. The Internet is in fact present to only about 3.5 per cent of the world's population, but those who are connected are able to use it to bypass the poor, and reach out to lucrative markets across the globe. As if to exclude the poorer nations further, 80 per cent of Internet sites operate in the English language, and even in the USA where the Web is taken for granted, the black community has only 7 per cent of the access.[5] We begin to see that the assets of globalization are not good news for everyone.

Scotswood is a neighbourhood in Newcastle, but it is in trouble. In this post-Fordist era the bottom has fallen out of heavy industry and ship-building, and global capital has been deftly moved to other parts of the world where labour and materials are cheaper. This has left Newcastle with wedges of very poor, unemployed communities, and Scotswood is one. It may be poor, but through generations there had grown up there the sort of close-knit and supportive community network that some would give anything for. In recent years Newcastle's 'Going for Growth' programme has attracted international capital for regeneration, and designer buildings are springing up where before there was only empty dockland and forgotten wharves. Scotswood stands right in the path of this development and therefore the local people had hoped to see regeneration coming their way at last. The local church, poor as it was, raised money to refurbish the church plant so that it could be ready for the promised 'New Jerusalem'.

What has happened however is the wholesale bulldozing of Scotswood and its church. The poor are being moved away, for the regenerated Scotswood will attract an altogether different class of people, with new skills, new lifestyles and high, taxable incomes. The old community of Scotswood, having taken generations to build, is demolished at a stroke. Multinational capital cuts itself wonderful deals by playing one city off against the next, going only to those centres where tax incentives are high and the standard of living for its executives promising. City politicians spend vast sums and expend all their energy competing for this investment – but that is time and money that before had been spent on education, welfare and the care of the poor. So with the shift on the part of the politicians from community management to entrepreneurialism, the result can be social fragmentation, unrest and, ironically, the eventual lack of an ability to compete for funds, since demoralized and fragmented players cannot win in an arena where any hint of lack of cohesion turns away investors.

The Reverend Nick Henshall, Vicar of Scotswood, has lived through the horrors of this situation with his people and has become a key figure in the political and spiritual battle that has been raging. In our conversations he tells me how helpful he has found an analysis of globalization. It explains why these disasters have fallen upon Scotswood and shows even more clearly that, at the heart of it all, is the very spiritual question of power.

Today, capital is held within a system of unregulated international competition, so towns, cities and national governments find themselves competing in an international marketplace for funds, trying to prove that they are the most attractive investment opportunity. Newcastle has set about this with a flare. Its 'Going for Growth' campaign has attracted considerable funding for the redevelopment of its ailing infrastructure, and that in turn is enticing international and national companies to establish themselves in the city. Similarly, London has its 'London First!' campaign and Leeds and Manchester have fought their way up the promotion ladder at the expense of other cities which have failed to win the battle for funds. Manchester has been so successful that it now has more venture capital providers than any other European city and the largest student population in Europe.

While some cities and towns win, others lose, and this results in tragedies too for our urban parishes. For while civic leaders concentrate on their role as creators of these profit-maximizing strategies, they far too often then forget their traditional role as funders of public utilities. This leaves the poor with declining support and care. Saskia Sassen has been able to calculate how this developing polarization 'just happens' to reinforce already extant divisions of class, gender and ethnicity. She challenges us with her findings: 'The uncomfortable question is whether the sudden growth in homelessness . . . the growth of poverty generally, the growth of low-wage employment without any fringe benefits, and the growth of sweatshops and industrial homework are all linked to the growth of an industrial complex orientated to the world market and significantly less dependent on local factors.'[6]

Shipbuilding, which sustained Newcastle in times gone by, has always been a somewhat mobile industry. In 1996 the *Guardian* reported that a ship, the *Sea Empress*, had spilt 65,000 tons of American crude oil into the sea just off the Welsh coast. The ship was Spanish built and registered in Cyprus, but flying a Liberian flag. It was managed from Glasgow but chartered by the French and captained by a Russian. Now shipbuilding itself has moved on from Tyneside and left Scotswood devastated. And today this can happen in almost any industry and at the drop of a hat – or the push of a computer button. The investment that Newcastle is now winning could just as easily and summarily leave again when profits prove more lucrative elsewhere. The investment which is redeveloping Scotswood may itself not remain long enough to sustain the new incoming community. And while the incomers may be on salaries commensurate with their global competitors, the manual skills of the present locals will be deemed largely superfluous, making sure that their salaries never keep up. So the gaps widens. Can any city or neighbourhood remain cohesive under these conditions?

But let us not sink into an unnecessary pessimism at this point. We must be careful not to accept globalization's myth that all power is now held in some nebulous centre away from all human influence. Kofi Annan, the General Secretary of the United Nations, in an address to the World Bank in 1997, referred to the paradox of globalization – that it offers tremendous benefits to some while simultaneously driving many into poverty and exclusion. It was, he said, a catalogue of 'squalor amid splendour'. With characteristic courage he then observed, 'the global dilemma of squalor amid splendour is a creature of human agency, and . . . it can be reversed by human agency!' Contrary to Margaret Thatcher's dictum, there is definitely an alternative, and the Christian faith is well placed to help humanity find it. Reflecting on the Newcastle situation, for example – the city officers and politicians could have acted differently. It is clear that they acted very badly towards the people of Scotswood, not consulting, keeping information back, and manipulating situations. Nick Henshall and what remains of his congregation have however now been able to make sure that a much closer and collaborative style of negotiation has become the norm. They have challenged the city leaders to question whether their competitive style was actually in their own long-term interest. Sometimes, when a congregation makes it clear it understands the councillors' predicament better than they do themselves, it can then steal a leading role in decision-making, and help in finding alternative strategies.

In March 1992 a prophetic cultural analyst, Benjamin Barber, wrote a paper called *Jihad vs. McWorld*,[7] in which he spoke first of the way that globalization makes us fall in line with its dominant preferences and styles of thinking. This is McWorld – the land of McDonald's, Starbucks, the mobile phone, and the American baseball cap – the ubiquitous signs of the imperialism of globalization. But human beings do not like being forced to give up their local ways, cultures and autonomy, and are angered when they are pushed aside by McWorld. This is why local cultures begin to hit back, says Barber, and create an intolerant and aggressive backlash – *Jihad* – as 'the last deep sigh before the eternal yawn of McWorld'. But Barber's article then becomes more optimistic. He believes that an alternative, participative democracy could grow from the bottom up, with ordinary people creating the climate and the determination to find new modes of solidarity and form democratic structures at every level of life. Barber was writing in 1992, and since then we have all heard about Islamic *Jihad* and American 'Crusading', but we are also beginning to see an upsurge in radical democracy building, much coming up, as Barber predicted, from local groups and organizations. There are educational and campaigning groups and individuals, networking to bring about a different style of life, and in this the Church and its congregations are playing a leading role. We need only think of the way a small group of Christian Aid thinkers built an international network called Jubilee 2000. Kofi Annan is right, there is an alternative.

New features of urban experience

For some of us, our local urban environment will look and feel much the same as it did in years past, and the changes and processes which we have described will seem rather remote from our everyday urban life and ministry. But globalization is speeding up many of the dynamics which have been around us for years, as well as adding new and significant features to the scene, and it is all creeping up on us, whether we notice or not.

Perhaps the most obvious impact is upon the built environment that surrounds us. A walk around today's city will alert the eye to the glass, steel and complex fascias of the new city centres. I stood recently with the rector of Hoboken, Geoff Curtiss, looking across the Hudson River towards Manhattan and was surprised to see a series of skyscraper buildings that looked so much like those of Docklands in London that I remarked upon it. Had the builders been using the same set of drawings? On exchanging details we realized that the same company, Olympia and York, was responsible for both developments although they are 3,000 miles from one another. Globalization is forcing its architecture upon the world, with shop-fronts, riverside and downtown high-rise developments that look the same the world over.

Developers tend to go for the easiest options, or 'soft targets', in order to make substantial and speedy profit when performing their 'plastic surgery' on cities. Usually the first to be targeted are the waterfronts, having been left to decline following the demise of shipbuilding or canal trading. Jim Abernathy, a Texan priest, took me to see the River Walk, in

San Antonio, the world's first example of waterside regeneration. The old river and canal now hum with Mexican guitars playing to happy tourists as they sip their tequilas. Back home in Birmingham I remembered how the adventurous Martin Hone opened his night club next to the canal in Gas Street Basin in the late 1960s. I returned recently to find a new world there, all rebuilt and humming with city restaurants, boutiques and people relaxing on the elegant canal bridges. There are over 3,000 miles of canal in England just waiting for the global developers to pounce. Other 'soft targets' for developers are the now empty manufacturing locations, industry having struggled with transportation and communication problems, eventually realizing that modern manufacturing technologies are better suited to outer areas. These inner 'brownfield sites' are targeted by government for development, but are not always so attractive to developers who may find the ground polluted and the tax costs prohibitive. As globalization speeds the process of industrial abandonment, however, these sites are bound to increase in availability. I was amazed to hear of the recent abandonment of São Paulo's vast automotive plant, only thirty years old but already deemed outmoded for modern production techniques.

At the other extreme many locations which have been hit by global forces attract little attention from developers at all, and are simply left to fend for themselves. When the coal mines of the Rhondda closed, the once bustling shops of Treorchy fell into decline and the heart went out of many of the people. The churches of the town found that their financial viability was hit as a consequence, but some opened re-skilling day centres and did their best to work with local initiatives to support families in crisis. In many areas, when the industry left, the population saw no reason to stay and the areas became ghost towns unable to sustain the infrastructure of local shops and schools, community clubs and services.

The building of Britain's new towns was a great boost to the confidence of post-war Britain, but some of these are also now beginning to feel their age. Basildon has celebrated its fiftieth birthday and is struggling to keep some of its housing stock fit for habitation. Margaret Thatcher allowed market forces into the council estates with her 'Right to Buy' policy, so many properties that are now privately owned stand out from the terraces because of their DIY improvements, new fascias and gates. Sometimes, it's quite the reverse, and the mortgage cost has crippled the purchasing family while the adjoining properties have been upgraded, with the privately owned property alone in disrepair. The current policy is therefore to transfer the housing stock into partnership management. Many developers and housing associations are geared up to work with local government, and the local community transfer entire estates out of local authority control and into the hands of newly formed local housing associations, locally managed and organized. David Eaton, Vicar of Vange in Basildon, has become the chair of the local company which now 'owns' and manages the housing on behalf of the tenants. The company is responsible not only for the tenancies but for community development, in the hope that residents will become proud of Vange, rather than continually aspiring to leave. David says that despite the headaches, there are obvious advantages over 'Right to Buy', as the estate is opened up to the possibility of real regeneration.

For others, it's not so good. The Broadwater Farm Estate got off to a bad start when the council and the builders did not even bother to employ an architect but just made it up as they went along. When Peter Robinson took me round his estate of Byker, on the church wall someone had scrawled 'God was 'ere'. The glory seems to have left the 'New Jerusalem', and so has the relevance of these estate communities to the new global economics. Even so, the people are still bombarded by the hard sell advertising of the global market and they will go to loan-sharks to purchase the commodities on offer – which only makes their alienation from the mainstream ever more apparent.

In America, outer estates are something else altogether. In the United States and now in Germany vast out-of-town estates have been specifically designed to be totally independent of the city which they satellite. These are the 'edge cities', and have to be seen to be believed. They house, employ and supply all the needs of their community and are no longer dependent upon the city at all. The trouble is that as everyone moves out to the edge cities the old city loses its sustainability. Houston, Texas has now so many edge cities that in the evenings the old city is almost dead – there is little to return to the city for. These edge cities are just as isolated from their parent city as our outer housing estates are, but unlike them they are certainly in the loop of the global economy and are doing very well out of it. I wonder if edge cities will come to Britain.

I mentioned earlier that many young, successful suburbanites choose to return to the towns and cities in order to be shot of the dreadful commuting, and to be nearer to the buzz and excitement of the cultural and leisure facilities on offer. Old terraced housing which is structurally sound is bought up by canny developers, 'gentrified' and then rented or sold to these incomers at highly inflated prices. This has been so successful that today even the lacklustre tower blocks of the 1960s are being bought up and upgraded in this way. Sometimes not only financial pressures but physical intimidation from developers move the old tenants out to make way for significant change in the locality. Either way, it's called 'social cleansing'. On occasion, the new neighbourhood works very well, and the small corner shops and local service industries can thrive on the mix of poorer and better-off local residents. Neighbourhoods become bustling and happy places once again, sporting street carnivals and fairs into the bargain. It's very understandable that these areas attract young and energetic people back from the suburbs, although recent research[8] shows that in most gentrified quarters the new residents are very privatized, 'eating out but not joining in'. Their children only socialize with other middle-class children, and there is little to no civic engagement, free time being spent with family, friends and on holiday. On the surface the neighbourhood looks more like a community again, but the reality can be very different.

Some of these old town and city quarters escape gentrification, but the international global processes affect them in another way. They become 'ethnic enclaves' where residents from ethnic minority groups live together to protect the economic, cultural and political well-being of their community. My own childhood home has benefited in this way, with High Street North now sporting some of the finest *sari* and *shalwar kameez* outfitters in Britain. My mother still lives in our old house, now surrounded by Hindu, Muslim and Sikh families, and although alien to her in many ways, she appreciates the sense of community and security they have built up as supportive neighbours. The *mu'azzin* calls the faithful to prayer, the smells of spice and curry fill the air and the local mini-cab firm commandeers every parking space.

Many of the old central areas are not gentrified nor do they become ethnic enclaves, but they can still become prey to the developers. As Rector of Poplar Parish, I became involved in the battle to safeguard the rights of local people when the London Docklands Development Corporation was commissioned by the government to attract massive office development. Enormous tax incentives brought the developers in but at a huge cost to the local community, who found themselves living in the heart of the biggest building site in Europe without compensation or voice. Ken Leech sums up the situation well: 'The lack of real (as opposed to rhetorical) consultation, the insensitivity to and, most of the time, contempt for, the local residents, the concern for profits more than for a good and wholesome community, the imaginative and visionary failures, the weakness of the transport infrastructure, and so much more, are integral to this history.'[9]

But the cockney spirit could not be dampened – 'these people have put the "con" back into consultation,' quipped Arthur. When the developers ran into financial difficulties they sought millions from the government, so the locals had a door-to-door collection and sent them a cheque for ten pounds, with love.

The opulence which the new globalized economy creates is staggering and the lifestyles we see flaunted in the modern city are astonishing. I was once driven around River Oaks, a wealthy quarter of Houston where they were advertising houses for sale 'in the low millions'. I was sorry to see so many lovely homes surrounded by high, defensive walls. One set of gates was festooned with welcoming Disney cartoon characters, but the attached notice read, 'These premises are always patrolled by armed security guards' – not so welcoming! But this defensiveness is not found only among the rich – some 50 per cent of private homes in San Francisco are now in 'gated communities', and the practice is fast developing in Britain. The intention is to allow the occupants to live in the city while isolating them from the dangers of the neighbourhood. Gated communities and segregated areas like this are appearing in cities and suburbs all around the world, dividing and fragmenting communities everywhere.

Many towns and cities have recently managed to attract universities and colleges to develop in their midst. This brings welcome life, bustle and prestige to the area, but again, the college campuses are often designed to segregate the young students from the wider community. Time and again, as the cities develop their new shape, we will see groups and communities segregated and increasingly divided one from another.

In order to attract wealth into the town or city, a great deal of central development is now geared for entertainment and delight. The town centre is 'Disneyfied' and turned into a site of consumption, with theme bars, international restaurant quarters, and cinemas. As the evening draws on, clubs attract the young from far and wide, who sometimes travel many miles at night to visit 'Party City'. But people are not only prepared to travel miles to work and play, but also to participate in post-modernism's meta-narrative, shopping. Britain is a nation of shopkeepers – obsessed with shopping. The UK now houses one-third of Europe's total retail space – we're born to shop! The British Airports Authority gains 60 per cent of its income from retail activity and so the company is classified no longer as a transport company but as a retail stock. The American shopping chain Wal-Mart has become so powerful that it now sports an information network second in the world only to the Pentagon. It has been estimated, but I cannot think how, that the average American sees 20,000 brand logos every day, each calculated to entice them to shop. In recent years half the Nobel prizes awarded in the field of economics have been to specialists in market psychology – no wonder we all want to shop. Once a week an early bus leaves Lincoln to travel to Lakeside, the shopping mall by the Thames, for a shopping day out! Once it was our parks and squares which displayed the statues of our heroes, symbolizing the values of the society – but now it is the privatized space of the shopping mall which displays our real treasures.

Neighbours

Recently, I was asked to act as one of the hosts for a group of bishops who were visiting an ethnic enclave for the first time in their lives. If they had not put themselves out to do so, they would never have had reason to visit such a place – and that goes for the vast majority of our population. While we may follow the soap opera *Neighbours* avidly, it's probable that we have no idea who lives next door, for globalization, contrary to its claim to bring us together, is isolating us one from another. Residents of the gentrified quarters, gated communities, ethnic enclaves, outer estates, and so on, can become quite isolated from other groups. We can live in our own little bubble, only meeting people like ourselves, without making significant contact with the 'other'. As incomes and wealth polarize at unprecedented rates, as people become frightened of moving out of their gated communities, as students remain with their friends, and faith groups all go to the same school, how will we ever get to know one another?

The old class divisions of our society have been dangerous enough, but this modern segregation means that it is becoming even easier for decision-makers to make important decisions about other communities without ever having to see or acknowledge the pain and suffering which their decisions create. Those who are benefiting from the new society may have no idea of how others, now locked away in other communities, are having to live their lives. Urbanologists refer to this phenomenon as the 'Dual City', where the rich become richer and more powerful, while the poor are pushed even further out on to the margins. Bill Kilgallon, once the Mayor of Leeds, knows his city well. He speaks of a 'two-speed city'. Leeds, he tells us, now has the largest internet server centre in Europe and its finance sector is making it one of the richest cities in Britain. Yet he wonders whether any of those who are benefiting know that in the poor quarters of their city the death rate for under-sixty-fives is 80 per cent above the national average. Urban people are segregated perhaps even more than ever before. Church life will mirror this segregation too, one congregation simply not being able to understand why other churches are not growing when they themselves are blossoming in all sorts of ways. They may not recognize that they are appealing to one sector of urban life, and their programmes and their worship may not be at all appropriate in another sector of this complex scene. 'One size fits all' becomes more and more untenable.

We need to note too that the very term 'urban ministry' is itself challenged by all that we have been describing. It is no longer possible, even if it were ever the case, to use a catch-all phrase like this and think that that specifies what sort of ministry one is engaged in. If we live in a predominantly suburban parish, the whole framework is urban to be sure, but it will be a very different ministry and a different life from the one lived in the ethnic enclave. However, there is another side to this, for the common use of the word 'urban' does serve to remind us that in reality we belong together. Although these barriers are threatening to separate us, our task must be to create new ways for people to acknowledge the gifts that others bring, and meet together to share them. Isolated segregation must not be the only urban story.

Therefore, one final question must be asked. Is it not a contradiction to say that globalization segregates us and at the same time brings people from around the world into closer proximity? To answer the question, ride the London Underground for a while and see different groups and types of people coming and going, colliding all the while. They inhabit the same space but, unless there is a strong indication that they are from the same group, it is very unlikely they will acknowledge one another. This constant meeting and not meeting is often referred to by urbanologists as the 'layered city', reminding us that although people from different classes and groups may come from their own segregated lives into similar spaces, to work, travel or to play for example, the degree of interchange and understanding which actually comes about during that time is not in any way as meaningful as the segregation which keeps their lives apart. This is a real challenge to the well-being of urban life but presents the Church with an opportunity to play a significant part in healing the wounds of a divided and segregated urban society. Christian ministers and congregations should learn that although global urban processes are dividing urban groups, and rural groups for that matter, ever more forcefully, the reality is that under God we belong together. We are responsible for one another and dependent upon one another. We should seek to heal the divisions, meeting to appreciate one another and working together to eradicate injustice and to share the delights of abundant urban living.

5 | Urban Meanings

From all that's gone before, we are now in a position to draw some conclusions about what all this global change means in the actual lives and experiences of urban people. The rush of the new urban processes has affected what our cities and towns actually look like – how the buildings and urban spaces are changing – but what of the soul of the people? How do we think, feel, worship and pray in an urbanizing world? What are our priorities? What do we believe about the places we inhabit? Where do we hope it all may be leading? What are the urban meanings?

Living urban lives

1. Urban change: nothing is assured

It's difficult enough being the minister of a poor urban church, often working with a small congregation, many of whom may be elderly or frail, but the situation is made all the more complicated by the flexibility and mobility demanded by the new global processes. When Rob turned up at St George's it was a great boost to the morale of the congregation because he volunteered to sort out the church accounts which had been getting into an ever greater muddle since Gladys died. The vicar was overjoyed until he was told by Rob that he would only be able to help for a few months because he was lodging with a friend and would soon move on.

The rapidity with which capital moves so that it can follow profit opportunities requires a very flexible style of company organization and a workforce accustomed to a different style of job patterning from that expected in former years. Time was when workers were respected for remaining with one company all their working life. Now it would be reckless to plan a life with that expectation. Employers in the up-and-coming industries prefer their workforce to job-hop because it keeps their team abreast of what advances are being made in competing companies. It introduces new blood and new ideas – and that is where the 'added value' originates which will create profits. Therefore, especially in the early stages of a working life, a young person will expect to move repeatedly from one company to the next and change location accordingly. Lifelong commitment no longer counts, whereas flexibility and mobility are essential for survival. No wonder then that personal relationships go the same way. Young people will often now opt to postpone thoughts of marriage, house ownership and family until much later in their lives when they can expect a little more stability. Until then they either live alone, have a series of partners or live with their parents, 'off and on' into their thirties.

Health and life expectancy have been enhanced by globalized medical research, so people in their late fifties and early sixties are now the new 'middle-aged'. More mobile younger people may come and go from a congregation, but the older set will remain to control the ongoing life of the church, making the style of worship and church activity reflect their preferences, referring to 1950s-style music as 'modern hymns' – not designed to convince the younger visitor.

The constant change and unpredictability of our new world brings its dangers. There was a time when a street-wise person would know how to 'talk down' someone in the street who was on the point of violence. Today, it's as well not to try, for they may be so drugged as to be totally unpredictable, and they may be armed. The way we expect society to cohere and make sense no longer applies. The impression given in *Faith in the City* is of a time when, if there was a breakdown in law and order, then the task was to restore urban society to its former harmony and balance. This rather nostalgic hankering after civility is still the base from which some clergy and congregations operate. But even if they ever did, urban communities don't work like that any more. Urban places, because of their very compacted nature, are always going to be contested spaces, so disagreement and urban conflict are inevitable. Our task must therefore be to create a framework of listening and mutual empowerment, so that the voice of the dispossessed can be heard above the fray. We have to find new methods of community negotiation which allow for the reality of conflict between groups and individuals rather than wishing it would go away. Everything is now contested, and change is here to stay.

Things have changed for the vicar too. To begin with, you can no longer rely upon people knowing who you are or how you fit into their world. I knocked on one door, dressed in black shirt and clerical collar to receive a ready welcome from the couple who grabbed their bag and came out on to the pavement with me. I was a little nonplussed until they asked, 'Well, where's your taxi?' The days when a vicar was automatically respected are also long past. Today, in a doctor's surgery or school, an excellent professional is still fair game for the violent and abusive, and the same goes for the clergy. There are vestiges of the old culture, but aggressive competition and thrusting confidence are the values that the new market processes encourage, and so one has to be ready for anything on the streets.

You can never be sure who you're meeting either. The Archdeacon of West Ham, Michael Fox, was chatting to two girls who had acted as servers at the Communion. Some way into the conversation they stopped him. 'Do you think we're both Indian?' One turned out to be from Trinidad where 30 per cent of the population are now Asian, and the other from North Africa. They all laughed because he could not possibly have known. In the city nothing is assured.

2. Finding an urban identity

The urban world has a habit of defining our identities for us even when we think it is making us free agents. In a world where market sales are everything, the brands go to great lengths to promote their own logos. They offer top salaries and status to those who help create consumer demand. Sports stars and entertainment celebrities all play their part in keeping the aspirations of the masses high enough to create the product consumption demanded by a system which has solved all the problems of production. The new economy has to change the personality of the urban population from being the 'metal-bashing' producers of yesteryear, who would have been proud of the sweat of their brow, into self-conscious consumers – the men too are having to learn to enjoy shopping! Advertising plays its part, as does the fantasy world of celebrities who act as the ultimate consumers and flag-flyers for the brands. The language, the dress, the driving style, the clubbing, and even the latté coffee, all become part of the new urban theatre of surfaces which serves the new consumer economics. So, whether you live in a gentrified terrace and drive a Lotus, or sit in a housing estate kitchen reading *Hello* magazine, the global market is controlling your urban lifestyle and helping to model your identity. I stood in the Lakeside Shopping Centre with one of the directors of a well-known retail company. He held up two white shirts and asked me, 'Which one is better quality?' The answer was plain, even for me to see. 'But we sell this other one for three times the price because it's got a brand label on it.' A shopper with her family had been listening in on the conversation and had to agree with the observation. She still took the substandard branded shirt. 'My lad won't be anybody if he doesn't have the right brand.'

Identity is given to us by our urban world in startling ways. The street culture of the alcoholic or heroin addict is part and parcel of the addiction. Their addiction gives them an identity and a place to belong. Football colours are worn by some boys and girls to give them a sense of belonging to something that matters and gives them an identity of importance. Young boys on the estate can grab the attention of their peers and earn the esteemed accolade – 'a Bad Boy'. The girls have to rely on brand clothing if they are to win status. A fifteen-year-old girl put it this way, 'It's like all the people in school and on the estate are all going mad about what the boys are doing – like rallying [joy-riding] and that – but no one really cares what we get up to, so we nick clothes every Sunday and that. So long as we're not slags.'

Young people are, however, very discriminating about their urban identities. In 2001, the ethnic enclaves of Oldham, Burnley and Bradford saw rioting gangs of Asian youngsters acting without regard to the guiding hand of their community elders. Up and down the country there had been an amazing conspiracy of silence for some years as self-appointed community leaders had presumed to speak on behalf of the very diverse Asian communities and groups. In return for their quietist style they had been feted by the white city authorities, just as long as they could guarantee to keep the lid on the communities. These self-styled community leaders were often given preferential funding for their projects, but this was resented by both the rising younger Asians and also by the local poor white communities. A multitude of other factors too converged to exacerbate the discontent, and the streets erupted. One lesson is clear – nobody, Asian, black or white, likes their personal or group identity to be presumed upon.

The Church feels the same. When I led the first church delegation to see the local leaders of the Thames Gateway regeneration project, we found the agenda had already been set for us. They assumed the Church would only be interested in sites for new church buildings and in caring for the elderly. It came as a surprise when they found that we wanted to talk about economic and environmental sustainability, jobs for local people and transport issues. They had presumed to know who we were and what our priorities would be.

A fast-moving urban world requires each of us to negotiate a whole series of identities, for there is a wide range of real and virtual identities on offer, requiring us to choose from any number of sub-cultural styles, sexual preferences, family and partnering lifestyles and presentations of ourselves. Surrounded by such complex choices and with few moral co-ordinates to guide, the urban person has to become very skilled in managing the expectations of groups which vie for allegiance. Each urban identity offers a kind of belonging in a frightening world, and each identity will have its own form of dress code, perhaps its own jargon or slang and an expected way of presenting oneself – all part of the urban theatre of surfaces.[1]

3. Urban relationships and meetings

We must not think of cities, towns or estates as simply 'places', as if they were containers of people and buildings. This is to misjudge how they tick. They are dynamic processes, or 'mesh-works' of interaction between people and groups, not 'fixed' but a moving dynamic of inter-relationships. The letter to the Hebrews tells us, 'there is no permanent city for us here' (Hebrews 13.14), for cities and towns are all in process, on the way – they change and adapt, like the people and groups who form them. Many urban people have travelled great distances to be where they now are. More than 130 million people now live outside their country of birth, and although some urban places, such as suburbia and the outer estates, tend to support mono-cultures, cities are so full of difference that this press of meeting can lead to tension and violence when not handled well. But many of today's generation delight in the vibrancy of cosmopolitan living, and listen with fascination to 'world' and cross-over music, enjoying international art and cuisine, and the whole kaleidoscope of cultures available in the modern urban centres. In 2002 the Queen's Jubilee was celebrated with a procession down the Mall by groups representing the cultures of the Commonwealth. It was fascinating to hear the music, see the colour and share the wonder of the cultures. Yet the TV commentators visibly struggled to understand how nearly all the participants could be British residents – and these commentators were opinion-formers of the British media! Meanwhile, the people of London were dancing on down the Mall, celebrating the cosmopolitan nature of their city, as never before.

When I grew up in the East End of London, the high street shops were run mostly by Jews and Chinese, but now Ken Leech tells us, 'The East End is one of the most racially mixed areas of the world. In 1991, 42 per cent of the population in Newham, and 36 per cent in Tower Hamlets, were from ethnic minorities . . . Over thirty-seven languages are spoken in east London.'[2] Some communities are used to getting on well together, while others can suddenly be at one another's throats. When the Bengali organizations decided to stage a great New Year Festival, the *Baishakli Mela*, some local Muslim groups were down on them like a ton of bricks. Liberal and 'radical' Muslims are just as antagonistic as are Irish Protestant and

Catholic Christians, and we do no one any service by being coy or romantic about these realities.

I sat with a group of Muslim men in Leeds just a few days after the terrorist attack in New York on 11 September 2001. They feared that white youths in particular had been sneering at the Muslim women in their *hijab* head-scarves and accusing any man wearing a turban or an Afghan hat of being a terrorist. The Muslim group had gathered regularly in a Methodist community centre, but had never met members of the white congregation there. We remedied that immediately, and soon had the women from both communities in intense and fascinated conversation. Meanwhile, in Basildon in the heart of white Essex, neighbours were prompted by the New York attack to share fears one with another, and this led to the first sustained meetings of Christians and Muslims that the county had known. Out of an evil act of terror, God creates opportunity for urban togetherness, mutual learning, and sharing of wisdom.

4. Urban spaces are tough places
When different groups meet in confined urban spaces, a great deal of power-brokerage has to take place. The chances of ever having peaceful urban harmony and consensus is remote – urban life is just not like that. Dealing with the press, planners and hard-headed politicians and corporate managers can prove a headache for an urban minister, but they can find us difficult too. If they offer us funding we are apt to accuse them of trying to buy us off, and if they don't offer us money then we adopt higher moral ground still. It must seem exasperating trying to negotiate with us.

The sheer geographical space can also cause tensions. Sometimes the restrictive geographical boundaries of the old British cities, drawn so long ago, are now crippling them economically, as the wealthy move across them to the outlying districts, taking their wealth with them. Of course the city's hinterland can lose out for other reasons. Many cities are now importing their food and services no longer from the locality but from thousands of miles away – it's estimated that on average each piece of food on our plates has travelled a thousand miles! – but the surrounding farms and agencies, which once formed the 'footprint' of the city, cannot compete for price and feel alienated from their local urban centre.

It is not easy for our youngsters to withstand the market pressures of acquisition and aggressive competition. They soon pick up the message and begin to think only about themselves. The schools are often oases of order and safety in a tough community environment, but some find it an up-hill struggle. A head teacher was away from school for the afternoon.

His departing advice to his staff was, 'Just try to keep the lid on everything till I get back.' Some of the children don't stand much of a chance because they start from such a low base – some teachers having to teach their six-year-olds basic skills such as speech and toilet training.

Some adults can't cope with being a 'loser' in this competitive achiever's culture so they call upon their GP to prescribe medication to ease the disappointments. Some turn to alcohol or heroin, and then have to support their habit with crime. Drugs are so tightly bound up with the criminal sub-class in urban culture that it is all too easy to find oneself, once on that path, descending to a life on the street where drugs are more freely available and where micro-arms and prostitution offer quick methods of affording them. Urban spaces are tough places.

5. Urban consumption

I'd always wanted to see the Houston leisure Astrodome. I had read that it uses as much energy to run its air conditioning units as is needed by a city with a population of 10,000 people. When I turned up I was shocked to see them demolishing it, in order to build a bigger one. Houston is so deregulated that it has sprawled out to fill 617 square miles. It has as much office space as London but half of it lies unused because it's cheaper to build afresh than to pay to maintain the older office buildings.

Our British roads are near to gridlock. I was reliably informed when I lived by the Blackwall Tunnel that it was one of the busiest roads in the world, but I always wondered how they calculated that, since rarely did a car manage to move along it. Central London traffic is now moving at an average speed of eight miles per hour, which is the same as that achieved by the horse-drawn carriages of the 1880s. Globalized bus companies, like Stagecoach, run buses through most of our town and city streets, but, because they are one-person operated they take more time for loading at each bus-stop, so creating expensive and polluting tailbacks. In Curitiba, Brazil, this bus problem has been addressed by the introduction of fast-loading bus bays and conductors.

We need to ask ourselves if the creation of so much waste and stress in the urban system and in the lives of urban individuals is worth the cost. A '24/7' lifestyle, relentless work-pressures, e-mail overload, and the cattle-truck grind of daily commuting, depletes the quality of life for millions. Children are driven the few hundred yards to school each day for fear of harassment, only to be driven home via the gym or sports field to get their weight down.

There is more to urban sustainability than pollution. Sustainable urban life requires social cohesion, jobs, quality education and health services, yet when I mentioned my concern for sustainability to the chief executive of a major British town, he replied somewhat ironically, 'Oh, we haven't got time for that sort of thing.' I sat him down with a team of local clergy and made him listen!

Perhaps the most basic question about urban sustainability is whether a town or city can remain stable when it is producing such inequality. The rich hide from the poor in their gated communities and the poor are angry because the city has been taken away from them by the wealthy. Both are alienated not only from one another but from the very cities and towns upon which they rely. To be sustainable our urban settlements have to have good governance, affordable homes, social inclusion, decent public services, and so on, so that the groups within them can contest their shared space without destroying it altogether.

6. Urban power: freedom or control?

One of the great myths of globalization is that it increases our choices. But in order to avail oneself of a choice in what is a market-driven environment, one has to have the money to turn that choice into reality. To choose the best school for your child, it turns out that one may need to have the wealth to live in its catchment area or pay the private fees – just another example of how the increasing division of our towns and cities into separate communities reduces people's options.

Our urban centres are inhabited by very powerful people whose choices control the lives of others. I have sat chatting long into the night with a chief executive whose only concern was to find a way to do the right thing for his town. On the other hand, I remember being invited by a high-flying PR consultant to a drinks and presentation party. She took me aside as if I were her 'good chum' and began sharing carefully crafted political indiscretions with me in order, I suspect, to win me over by thinking I had now become one of the people 'in the know'. It made me feel quite sick. There is a lot of sleaze around, despite the best efforts of so many good people.

Often the problems are not so much with the people as with the systems they operate. The slow, grinding bureaucracies of some local authorities is renowned. In the 1960s, it was obvious that only white people were obtaining council house tenancies, but it was not until the 1976 Race Relations Act that anything could be done about it. Likewise, the system of competitive bidding for extra regeneration funds seems to offer real opportunities to all urban regions to put their case. What actually happens, however, is that those who already are strong enough to make good applications win the funds, and those who fail feel even more de-skilled and demoralized.

So it is that time and again urban culture offers the illusion of amazing choice and freedom but actually majors on control. The Romans used 'bread and circuses' to keep the populace from asking questions, and we are given shops and entertainment. But urban life is still dominated by controlling CCTV surveillance, interminable bureaucracy, mortgages, phone-codes, social expectations, traffic lights and timetables. The Church will have to work hard to educate people for freedom – for we urban citizens are more used to being controlled than we think we are.

7. Celebrating the urban

David Richards, Vicar of St John's, Stratford, was hailed from across the road by his Roman Catholic colleague. 'I was sixty on Sunday!' It only transpired later that he was not talking about his birthday but the fact that he could now number sixty different nationalities in his congregation – really something to celebrate! I was anxious that my family once had to billet for a while at the Seamen's Mission in the heart of Poplar. It was known as one of the toughest places in the East End. But I should not have worried – we all had a wonderful time and the hospitality was over-whelming. Some years later we decided that nevertheless it would be good to set up a Neighbourhood Watch scheme for the local streets. Bernie was a great community man so he was elected as secretary. He was out front cleaning his taxi one Saturday when a lorry drew up with a team to take the scaffolding down from the adjacent block of flats. Bernie spent the afternoon making them cups of tea and chatting with them. On Monday morning the real builders arrived to ask if he, as Neighbourhood Watch co-ordinator, knew where all their scaffolding had disappeared to! The only way the community knew how to deal with the situation was to throw a grand party for him, so that he wouldn't feel so embarrassed.

Life in a challenging urban environment, despite all the problems and worries, gives us so much to celebrate. Time and again the presence of the living God shines through, transforming situations and people. A Leicester curate said of his time on a tough housing estate, 'It felt like having my hands tied and being thrown into a furnace, but instead of being consumed, the flames burnt through my fetters.'

If you don't enjoy a celebration, it's best not to go into urban ministry, because there people really know how to party. There is something of the eucharistic spirit deep in the heart of such communities. I love the city and enjoy giving thanks for it – giving thanks for all the employment, wealth creation, housing, architecture, artistic achievement, the supportive services, cosmopolitanism and energy. The city can be full of vitality, full of experiment and invention, be outward looking, expansive, industrious, and open to the world at large – offering hope for the future. Urban environments present us with their problems and their challenges, but they also offer us their splendour.

Finding ways to respond

Having told the urban story from the perspective of the Bible, the academic disciplines and from the point of view of our Church's ministry and mission, we have recognized that during recent years there have been changes as we have been impacted by the economic and social forces of globalization. This analysis of the urban scene leaves us with a rich tapestry of description and understanding. Such an awareness will now allow us to reflect theologically, by reference to our Christian traditions of Bible, worship, prayer and church life, so that we can determine how best to respond to the urban challenges.

We must remember of course that globalization is still a contested concept and that is why we have not, in this analysis, assumed that *everything* in the world is determined by the market, as the globalization mind-set would have us believe. Some would question globalization itself, arguing that because 'imperialism' has had such a bad press, it has had to change its brand name to 'globalization', to make us feel easier when having to do everything 'the American way'. The prophetic American commentator, Galbraith, has asked, 'Does Globalization exist or has it been invented to allow the politics of economic entry into other countries?'[3] Be that as it may, our question remains, how to respond to our urban situation now that we have a more accurate picture of it – for respond we must. The Church Council meeting may be taken up with discussion about the new hymn book, but they will not find it easy to ignore the homeless addicts who are taking over the churchyard, nor the kids who are trying to steal the amplification system, nor the mentally ill woman who sits at the back of the church crying all through the service. For an urban Church the issues of health, poverty, illiteracy, employment, and so on, simply will not go away. An urban Church Council is compelled to make choices about these issues and cannot pretend not to know. One way or the other, we must respond.

So what can the urban Church do? First, it has its tried and tested responses of pastoral care and loving service to those in need. There are many saints and unsung heroes and heroines working in countless congregations and Christian projects across Britain, changing people's lives and circumstances for the better and giving them new hope and supportive comfort. Being of service to others also has a way of healing the helper, for every time we offer support and love to someone in need we are in turn blessed by them. They give us new insights, and an integrity we would not otherwise have. In addition, good pastoral care makes us listen, for we become personally touched by the experiences of those who are at life's hard edge. When you sit through the night with a homeless couple, telephoning round, desperately trying to find them a place for the night without success, and the next morning you hear the news that the town's homeless are now well catered for, you don't accept the myth any more. Pastoral care changes our perceptions. It may not change the world and address the causes of every problem, but it often does change someone's world for the better, and for that, we thank God.

Compassion, care and loving service are wonderful qualities, but they are attributes which we thankfully share with all humanity. There is however something in addition to pastoral care – and not instead of it, I hasten to add – which the Christian faith can bring which is distinctive, and we must hasten to bring it. I want us to be ambitious for the gospel, and my hope is that listening carefully to the new urban situation will help us discern precisely what that Good News is for our generation, and help us act on it.

The Revd Benny Hazlehurst, a leading urban practitioner, wrote to me following a meeting we had both attended in south London. He wrote,

> For me one of the real challenges of the Gospel is that in his ministry to individuals, Jesus managed to challenge the structures and perceptions of those around him in such a powerful way. In many ways, starting with the micro, Jesus profoundly disturbed the macro, and that is something which moves me deeply . . . When I was at university I was heavily involved with Christians who fed me the line how important it was to bring people to Christ while they were there, because they would become the economic and political leaders of tomorrow. However I found no parallel to this in Jesus' ministry and instead read things like the Nazareth manifesto, and passages about Jesus' constant concern for the poor and the destitute.
>
> I only began to see the alternative some years later in Hong Kong working with drug addicts, the homeless, etc. The theology of the group I was working with was that God calls us to minister to the

poor, the marginalised, the oppressed; and that when we minister effectively to the poor, the rich sit up and take notice. The problem is that all too often we don't minister effectively among the poor anyway, and the rich and powerful remain unchallenged and unimpressed by the Gospel we proclaim . . . What we must do, it seems to me, is creatively and critically to engage with these forces at every level, being both prophetic and innovative, as we try to encourage and instil the values of the Kingdom of God into the process of continuous change. That is not to 'soil our hands' as some would claim, but to live out the incarnation of Christ in this day's society and world.

Andrew Davey puts the same challenge in another way by asking how it might be that local pastoral praxis becomes simultaneously global political praxis.[4]

I have found it very helpful, when struggling with the critical question of how we turn our urban analysis into Christian action, to look at the writings of an Italian thinker who was coming at things from a very different perspective, but who nevertheless gives us some very good pointers. Antonio Gramsci[5] was held in prison by Mussolini just as Fascism was taking control of the minds and hearts of the Italian people. Gramsci was worried about the way in which Mussolini was using the power of culture and ideology – through the press, the Church, education, the military and so on – to control the popular mind-set. He argued that, by controlling the culture of society a government could win and retain the consent of the people upon whom they were imposing their regime, however dreadful. Both Mussolini and Hitler used rhetoric, the arts and great cultic gatherings to convince the people that there was no alternative. Gramsci was clear, however, that culture is an arena of struggle and contest, in which we have to engage in order to prove that there is an alternative to oppression.

Cultural assumptions, be they good or bad, can be formed by all sorts of processes and pressures, and because cities and towns are such powerful places, they can pattern our mind-set in very decisive ways. Culture and cities go together. It seems that the Sumerians, the first city builders, also invented writing in about 3000 BCE, using it to mark their city boundaries. The development of writing was not merely coincidental with the rise of city life but helped to make it what it is. The city is full of symbols and cultural pointers – indeed it is 'writing' in its most sophisticated and aggressive form – telling us what it is, and what it means. One learns to 'read' a city as one walks around it, noting a building here or some creative graffiti there, spotting a deserted building site and a terrace of houses being gentrified. But it is not only by its built environment that a city proclaims its symbolic nature. Tourist maps and guide books, the stories that the locals tell, the parades and festivals, political events and significant personalities – all merge to create the city as a 'text' to be read, as a symbol of its own dominant values, its joys and misgivings. Steve Latham, a Baptist from Paddington, talks in similar vein when he describes the discipline of urbanology as 'a mystical exercise in which you intuit the spirit of the place'.[6] This is why some cities become so symbolic that we need only hear their name to find that they represent to us a whole host of meanings – just think of Babylon, Berlin, Zurich and Jerusalem. Today, 'urbanism' – that urban mind-set that floods across the globe – has a cultural power to influence people far and wide. But only if we are aware of how these controls occur and dominate our thinking and our ways of life can we hope to rise above them and become conscious of the alternative.

We have to find ways of helping people to ask important questions of their society – to move from what they know full well from the culture which surrounds them, to a point where they become conscious that there could be another, and better, way for society to behave. And the person who will best teach us how to do this is Jesus of Nazareth.

Time and again Jesus tells a tale from people's everyday experience, but then in the final few words of his story, he will spin the whole matter on its head so that his hearers will be left asking questions – and become conscious that, contrary to popular opinion and the cultural mind-set, there is an alternative. Sometimes Jesus will offer a story which gently opens up the alternative. He tells them that a wise person will do well to search and search for the lost coin or the pearl because what they have now simply does not compare. In another case he tells of a man who, having been attacked and left by the road, was left to die because the Temple culture demanded that the priest and the Levite should pass by on the other side and not touch blood on their way to worship. This they knew – this was the cultural mind-set to which there was no alternative. But then Jesus opens up the situation to question, and he leaves his listeners with a problem – 'But who proved to be the neighbour?'

No doubt, when the rich young ruler came to ask Jesus what he should do to inherit eternal life (Luke 18.18–23) he was blind to the way in which he held his wealth at the expense of others. To begin with, Jesus offers him, in conformity with the contemporary opinion, the expected answer to his question: 'Keep the Commandments'. But the young man is not satisfied and wants to dig deeper and become more fully aware of his predicament.

He prompts Jesus to go further. Jesus therefore points out that although the rich man may not be aware of what he has been doing, the only complete answer to his predicament is to withdraw himself from a situation in which his wealth has been the cause of others' suffering. 'Sell all that you have and give it back to the poor . . . and follow me.' But a full awareness of how his accepted way of doing things had led to such misery for others was just too much for him to bear, and he 'was overcome with sadness, for he was very rich'. Jesus constantly encounters people and opens up their awareness so radically that it demands of them a complete turn-around – a repentance – and a reformulation of the social processes that govern their relationships with society. Jesus confronts his contemporaries by telling stories, but he also lives the alternative life which he proclaims. He gathers disciples around him in order to create the new community of awareness. It will be a new order, a new society, and he will call it the 'Kingdom of God'.

Part 3

The Jesus Challenge

Reflections in the light of the Kingdom

6 | Jesus, His Mission and His Praxis

The first part of this book considered the stories of our urban experience, and the second analysed the present urban scene, acknowledging how things have moved on apace within recent years. Having accomplished those two tasks it is now possible to move towards the third element of what it is to 'do theology', namely theological reflection. Just as generations have done before us, we have to ask the theological and missional questions afresh in relation to the specifics of our own context having now analysed it, and we recognize that Jesus has given us ways in which we can undertake this theological critique. His parable stories have a built-in dynamic. They demand of their hearers that they look with fresh eyes to the assumptions of their age and contrast those with the principles of the new society which he inaugurates – the Kingdom of God. He uses his parables to make us look and understand but then expects us to change our ways, repent and believe the gospel. With Jesus, theological reflection involves critique, offers an alternative, and demands change – and all this only after thirty years of situation analysis.

As Jesus goes about his mission we see change occurring all around him, as he offers to those he encounters a new way of being and living. He creates a discipleship community in which the new life culture is one of being together under God's love and forgiveness. In every aspect of his ministry, in all that he says and all that he does, he is giving them signs of this new way of being with others and with God. His actions are more than signposts to this new society, for they actually participate in that to which they point. With him it's as if this new society under God has actually begun – indeed he inaugurates it and calls it into being. When Jesus enacts his sacramental signs of healing and transformation, it's not just 'me meeting Jesus' but all the ground rules for society are made to change, to conform to the principles of this new way of being together. It is a profound cultural and societal shift that has affected the individual at the very deepest level, but at the same time it has changed the whole balance of history!

And for us, the beauty of it all is that as we in our day read the biblical accounts of how Jesus brings this about among his disciples, so the Holy Spirit breathes into our own creative imaginations ways in which that may happen afresh for us too and then empowers it to happen. So in the third part of this book we will look at the Jesus story and ask the Holy Spirit to continue that divine act in us, in our urban mission and ministry.

Jesus and the Kingdom

Jesus taught that his new society under God will entail significant changes in how we see and experience everything. It is this right vision which will help elicit repentance within us and so lead to right action. He therefore speaks of the forgiving inclusivity of the father at the return of his prodigal son. He points to the way that loving action can cut across the barriers of race or tribe, in the parable of the Good Samaritan. He warns of the crisis awaiting those who failed to care, in the stories of Dives and Lazarus and the sheep and the goats. He points to a new style of leadership as he rides a donkey into Jerusalem, and proclaims a new time of holiness as he throws the money-changers from the Temple. While each of these, in itself, is such a small mustard seed of an action in the face of the global might of the Roman Empire, nevertheless each is significant of a new culture, a new way of being, a new logic, a new society whose participants will change the world radically. And all this he calls the 'Kingdom of God'.

'Kingdom' is a word which, of course, should cause us problems for it summons up notions of domination and subservience, masculine power and territorial claim. Jesus' hearers seem initially to have made such assumptions. But Jesus, as we shall see, intentionally uses the word in order to subvert it, deconstruct it and redefine it – 'My Kingdom is not of this world!' The Gospels indicate that in every aspect of his ministry, Jesus is emphasizing the significance of this 'Kingdom of God'. In his preaching Jesus proclaims, 'The time is fulfilled, and the Kingdom of God has come near; repent, and believe in the good news.' In his ministry, 'Jesus went about all the cities and villages, teaching in their synagogues and proclaiming the good news of the Kingdom and curing every disease and every sickness.' He prays, 'Thy Kingdom come', and on his cross is emblazoned the inscription, 'The King of the Jews'. He sends out his disciples with the commission, 'as you go, proclaim that the Kingdom of Heaven is close at hand', and he tells them that at the final judgement those who care for the oppressed will be rewarded, with the words, 'take as your heritage the Kingdom prepared for you . . . for I was hungry and you gave me food'. At every turn of his ministry it is to the Kingdom that Jesus points.

Justice, forgiveness and justification are clearly central to it, and yet, when asked to describe this Kingdom, Jesus prefers not to say precisely what it is, but tells stories of what 'it is like'. Stanley Hauerwas, the American theologian, talks of Jesus presenting the Kingdom of God as a story or drama in which we are invited to play a part. We must act both faithfully and creatively – keeping the story going, holding to the plot, but being open to surprises at every turn. Each Kingdom parable requires us to work with the story and enter into it as an active enterprise of reflection and action. In this way we will learn that the only way to understand the Kingdom's concept of justice is to experience it for ourselves, by doing justice and walking humbly with our God. To know what love is, we must experience love for ourselves. So as Hauerwas says, 'We do not learn what the kingdom is by learning of freedom and equality; we must first experience the kingdom if we are to know what kind of freedom and what kind of equality we should desire.'[1] It is this 'taste' of the Kingdom which then gives us the confidence to enter further into the Kingdom's field of influence on our journey of faith. We find that by living out the Kingdom's vision in this way, we create the very atmosphere and conditions in which the radical new alternatives can be realized. 'The claim of the parable is that the Kingdom is at hand; the challenge of the parable is that the Kingdom can only be perceived when it is performed.'[2] In our urban ministry we may often find that we only glimpse the Kingdom as we perform it, but that glimpse is enough. Mavis has been bedridden in Southend for years, and misses her garden dreadfully. Her local community have therefore rallied round and painted her bedroom walls with all her favourite flowers and filled every available space with a flower pot. The painting is not all that professional, but the smile on Mavis's face is a glimpse – just a tiny glimpse – of the breaking in of the Kingdom of God.

If we find ourselves in ministry in a tough urban location it is very easy for us to become despondent, feeling that our tiny efforts are of no account. We may be able to set up a small group for addicts or offer a tiny Eucharist for the poor each week, but all the odds for change seem against us. In these circumstances we remember that when Jesus told his disciples that they would always have the poor with them, he was acknowledging the limitation and particularism of the human condition. Even his own incarnation brought those limitations. One man in first-century Palestine could not feed all the hungry of the world, but once that was acknowledged, Jesus could then make sure that his every act – his miracles, his sacraments and parables – whilst inevitably particular to that time and place, were each symbolic and sacramental of the universal Kingdom. The contemporary slogan says, 'Think globally and act locally', but Jesus' local actions actually *participate* in his universal Kingdom, so it is better to say that he was acting *and* thinking both locally *and* globally – indeed universally!

Now we begin to understand that the word 'praxis' – the interaction of action and reflection – can, with Jesus, have an even fuller meaning. The levels at which Jesus' praxis is operating include the local, the global and the universal, and if universal then this means that his praxis extends through time and into the future. Jesus' sacraments already participate in the Kingdom of God yet to come, just as our own local urban Kingdom actions can participate, to some extent, in effective global change. When Jesus describes his mission in Luke 4.18, he quotes the prophecy of Isaiah, 'He has sent me to preach good news to the poor, to proclaim release to captives.' The fact that Jesus was alongside the poor in this way was of course a sign of his concern for their plight, but also a crucial sign that the Kingdom was at hand and that the future was under judgement. We are seeing the signs of a future Kingdom now!

Michel de Certeau[3] believes that while the powerful have strategies, the poor can only have tactics, but the Jesus praxis offers us signs of a Kingdom where this no longer pertains. His Kingdom offers to the poor tools by which they can fully participate in bringing about the future. In all that Jesus teaches us about the Kingdom of God, one aspect shines through as particularly important, and that is the role the poor play at the centre of its dynamic, both now and into the future. This is very significant for those in urban ministry – just as it will be for those ministering in areas of deep rural poverty. In the New Testament, just as in the Hebrew Scriptures, the poor are God's especial treasure. They are looked down upon by others and even blamed as if their poverty were punishment for their sin. Juvenal, in the early second century, wrote 'If you are poor you are a joke . . . what a laugh if several patches betray frequent mending!'[4] But with the coming of the Kingdom Jesus tell us that people in this position will be vindicated – 'Blessed are the poor!' – and will be seen to have played a special part in the drama of salvation. Jesus bids us therefore stand alongside the poor so that we may be better placed to seek the Kingdom and respond positively. If the Gospels teach us that the poor are indeed the first subjects of the Good News and play this crucial part in the Kingdom, then this will demand considerable repentance and transformation on our part. The

Church as we know it will have to change, for we recognize how, despite our best efforts, the Church has often had its eye on success rather than on poverty.

The social and economic status of Jesus and his family has been variously argued, but I am convinced that his skills in the construction and building technology of his day would have placed him above the very poor on the financial scale. Jesus therefore must have made a conscious decision to work alongside the poor, downtrodden and disaffected, and he expected his disciples to follow suit – 'we have given up everything to follow you' (Matthew 19.27). He throws open his Kingdom to those who by traditional and contemporary standards were considered unclean and of no account, and sets them at the very centre of its affairs. He takes children and women, the blind, the lepers and the destitute and speaks to their concerns and offers them inclusion. Jesus does not simply afford them dispassionate justice but aggressively positive discrimination. We see this very clearly in his parable of the labourers in the vineyard, for the dispassionate logic of our market economy sees no justice at all in paying the same wage to poor labourers when they have worked varying hours. But there is divine justice in sharing equally with all the poor the benefits of the alternative Kingdom society, independently of how much they have worked, for the divine economy of the Kingdom rests on abundant generosity and a justice which is far from dispassionate.

This is a call to stand with the poor even though there is no hint at all in the gospel that poverty is *in itself* good – it may be embraced as a means to an end, but that end is a world in which 'there will be gifts for you: a full measure, pressed down, shaken together, and overflowing, poured into your lap' (Luke 6.38, NJB). Indeed, we are not arguing here that wealth or capitalism are in themselves malevolent, for the profit motive has proved its worth in providing a fallen world with wealth-creation and high economic standards of living from which we are pleased to benefit. Jesus makes an option for the poor, knowing that in this way the rich too can be saved from the injustice in which they are trapped. For the problem of poverty is beyond both the poor and rich alike – our fight is not just against rich unjust individuals holding on to power and privilege, but against complex global and urban processes which incline them to do so.

This is why the letter to the Ephesians says, 'our fight is not against flesh and blood but against the powers and principalities of this dark age' (Ephesians 6.12). While not denying the burden of responsibility which every human being carries, we know that the urban poor are not the only cause of their problems — they are much more sinned against than sinning! But it would be false to lay the blame on each and every rich person as if to say that there was never a rich person who did not act justly or sacrificially. We are all in this dilemma together, and together we must seek for liberation and forgiveness for all. Our urban mission must therefore be open to all people of goodwill – but the guiding rule of our strategy must be God's option for the poor. But this is a testing option and we soon find out that being with the poor and vulnerable is not easy.

I very well remember agreeing with Big John that I would meet him in the White Hart to talk his problems through. I arrived somewhat later than expected and so had to push my way through a crowd of rowdy young men to get to the bar to ask the landlord if Big John was still around or had left a message for me. Suddenly I felt a tug on my belt and found myself being hauled backwards into the centre of the gang of lads. They pulled my clerical collar off and, assuming that a priest had to be gay, began to hit me and accuse me of being Big John's boyfriend. I managed with great difficulty to fight my way to the door and ran away, hurt and terrified. What frightened me more than anything however was the very fear itself and the intense experience of vulnerability at the hands of those drunken young men. But that night I learnt for the first time in my life the vulnerability which any gay man lives with from day to day – and saw the issue of sexuality from an altogether different perspective. I had read all about it, but now I 'knew'.

Urban ministry alongside the poor will assist us as Church to fight against the Church's greatest temptation, which is to consider itself a community of insiders who have the answers. Being with the poor will make us see ourselves for what we really should be – the Jesus community of outsiders. From this perspective upon the world we will see more clearly who is truly benefiting and at whose expense – and we will be given the heartache to engage the issues more courageously.

Urban life and ministry help us to learn the Kingdom by experience. The Word of God is not an abstract principle – it is not merely letters written on the pages of the Bible. The Word of God comes to us as the living Person of Jesus Christ manifesting love and justice in a harsh world. In order to inaugurate the Kingdom of God, the Word of God came in flesh and blood through a young Palestinian girl in the first century, in a place both politically dangerous and spiritually tortuous. 'He came to his own,' says St John, 'and his own people did not accept him.' His Kingdom was so at odds with human society that at its coming we witness a culture clash of global dimension. Jesus immediately has to enter into a cultural battle with the world – a struggle for hearts, minds and bodies – so that the values of the Kingdom of God may prevail, and the light shine out in the darkness. 'The time is fulfilled,' he proclaims, 'and the Kingdom of God is close at hand. Repent, and believe the gospel.'

Culture and context

Before we can move our theological reflection on, it will be important for us to look more carefully at how we are using the words 'culture clash' and 'culture', and to see why context and culture are so very important to Jesus and to the victory of the Kingdom of God. Let me address the matter in this way.

Human beings are very complex, sophisticated and vulnerable animals. Our 'formation' is therefore more subtle and takes a great deal longer than that of other creatures. As babies and children, our period of education and preparation for life is at the hands of others who have trodden this way before, and through the course of generations have constructed for us a complex network of norms of behaviour, and more than that, a framework of thinking and conceiving which allows us to register the world around us in manageable ways. This sophisticated framework includes markers like language, dress, household and religious taboos, relational protocols, family and tribal networks, and much more. This framework of symbols, meanings and norms, we call 'culture', and the function of a culture is to help human beings to make some sense of all the possibilities and challenges which come their way – so that they do not feel cast off alone on a sea of chaos.

Different groups of course will construct different cultures, and over many generations our particular culture will most certainly expect us to make sense of the world in its own particular way. This has a profound impact upon our personal identity and our sense of identity as a group, making the interplay of person and culture very complex indeed – as Rabbi Jonathan Sacks says, 'Where does my identity stop when I shake hands with another?' This means that our culture is of immense importance if we are to grapple with the question of personhood. The 'Who am I?' question will always have to involve the 'Where am I?' question. It also implies that one's cultural context is an arena which can be acted upon and changed, and this is precisely what Jesus is intent on doing. Jesus is proposing a new frame of reference to live our lives by – a change of personal identity and a change to a whole new culture and mind-set, called the Kingdom of God.

But Jesus is not the only one seeking to bring about cultural change. Written across our local high streets we now see the same advertisements, the same shop-fronts, fashions, logos, and companies – McDonald's, Stagecoach and IBM are everywhere imprinting their cultural norms upon the urban landscape. And it's not only the high streets that bear these new cultural marks. We all know for example that we have to get into a certain 'way of thinking' if we are going to work with the computer technology of Microsoft Word. This global company expects us to think in its way – it conforms us to its culture. Go to the Wal-Mart website and it will tell you all about its 'company culture' as the biggest store in the world. So the engines of globalization are themselves 'culture carriers' seeking to create a frame of reference for the way we can live our lives and think our thoughts. Urban culture is writ large across the world, and when we 'read' a city, that city asks us to read it, mark it, and inwardly digest it. It seeks to conform our identity to its culture.

Globalization has not however written its text on to a blank screen. Each urban area, be it the city, the industrial or housing estate, the town, suburb or large village, has a history of its own, a story to tell and a particular people who live there. As we seek to read it, we will find that there are sub-texts from cultures that were there long ago, or perhaps still persist. There will be graffiti from the past and the present, scrawled into the language and pre-dispositions of the people. The family styles and personal relationships, the leisure and the group dynamics, will all echo to sub-cultural frames of reference over which globalization tries to write its conforming gloss. This is why, when we read an urban culture, it is very important to read both its dominant global culture and its own local life, so that we can analyse the power dynamics which operate within and between the cultures which make it what it is.

We become so used to our own culture that we lose the ability to see it and to appreciate its controlling power over us. Whoever it was who discovered water, it was certainly not a fish, for water is the only culture it can conceive of. Because a culture has such power to control without us ever knowing that it is doing so, it is necessary to train our minds to critique the culture that surrounds us so that we may become more aware of why we find ourselves making the decisions we do and why it is that we relate to one another in particular ways. Because of this immense power to control, we might say that a culture not critiqued is the most dangerous thing on earth. And that is also why a Godly culture is the most beautiful thing on earth – and Jesus taught us to call it the Kingdom of God.

A major part of the culture which dominated Palestine in the time of Christ was one which was written in the mode of institutional religion. There was therefore no critiquing or gainsaying the local culture without appearing for all the world to be denying the ordinances of God. As soon as Jesus began to critique that dominant culture, he must have known that he was in for trouble. His very use of the phrase 'Kingdom of God' was subversive of that culture, for the brutal Herod had been allowed to call himself 'King of the Jews' by the Roman authorities and he ruled his kingdom with a cruelty which is hard to credit. Jesus took his word 'kingdom' and deconstructed it – 'my kingdom is not of this world' – and began to give it totally new and therefore subversive meanings. It would be a heavenly Kingdom of God – one of forgiveness, justice, mercy and inclusion – made all the more remarkable by its uncompromising contrast with the kingdoms of this age, both of the Caesars and the Herods.

In order to build this new Kingdom and bring about this profound cultural change, Jesus begins to engage in a courageous ministry of transformation by word and action and inspires us to do the same. But where will we get the strength or the wisdom to carry it off? St John's Gospel tells us that after the resurrection, the disciples were confined 'behind closed doors for fear of the Jews' – those who controlled the powerful Jerusalem culture. Jesus then came into their midst and showed them the marks of his crucifixion. He commissioned them and gave them the power to engage as never before, by breathing on them the gift of the Holy Spirit. This Spirit of God is like a rushing wind – it 'blows where it pleases; you can hear its sound but you cannot tell where it comes from or where it is going. So it is with everyone who is born of the Spirit' (John 3.7–8). If we receive this gift of the Spirit, we will be opened to these possibilities of imaginative wisdom and freedom which we would never have anticipated.

Also, the Spirit gives us such hope! It is a hope for the future which empowers us to live now 'as if' the Kingdom is already here, for in many respects it is – glimpsed and experienced already in the lives of those who are 'born of the Spirit'. This future Kingdom reference provides us with such a determination and realistic optimism that we simply cannot be beaten by the present. It gives us a determination which helps us punch above our meagre weight – and we find ourselves moving mountains. When we went with some trepidation as a small Anglican delegation to the New York offices of the United Nations we never expected that we would be met by Mr Nitan Desai, the United Nations Under-Secretary General. We should have had more confidence in the power of the Kingdom, for we had come to talk about addressing the injustices of our global cities, and to such a Kingdom issue he was more than keen to respond.

We can have this confident faith in the future of the Kingdom because we see glimpses of it so very close at hand. But the advent of this Kingdom demands response – 'The time has come, the Kingdom of God comes near, repent and believe the Good News' (Mark 1.15, NJB). The word 'repentance' is often taken to mean 'saying sorry' but that really misses the point. It translates the Koine Greek word *metanoia*, which more literally means 'having an alternative mind'. So when Jesus asks for repentance, he expects us to take on a new mind-set and make an active commitment to a whole new frame of reference for our lives. Time and again we see Jesus helping his disciples to repent, find this new mind-set and turn their lives around. When a paralysed man is lowered into the middle of his gathering by four friends, Jesus uses it as an opportunity to question the received cultural wisdom and call people to this *metanoia*-repentance. Jesus heals the paralysed man – which is exciting enough – but then he makes a point of telling him to pick up his bed and walk, no longer dependent on those who had brought him. It is transformation for the paralysed man, but there is a lot of change in store for his friends too. Now they must release him to be his new healed and independent self. Much of our urban ministry can unfortunately leave people where we found them, helped but still dependent upon those who helped them. Such people know what a burden it is to be carried and to have their future and their identity set by others. It is a culture of dependency which infects so many poor areas – urban and rural alike. Without *metanoia*-repentance on our part – a new Kingdom way of being and thinking – our urban programmes of help and care for others will turn out to be just more of the same: dependency by another name. The paralytic will still have to be carried by his friends.

Urban Palestine in the first century

Some may think that Jesus' teaching about the Kingdom of God is somewhat unrealistic and impractical in the face of what we now have to contend with. While Jesus lived a simple peasant life, we are confronted by the complexities of modern city or town life, challenged to carry out our mission amidst a plethora of sub-cultures, all overlaid by the complex processes of globalization. But if we think that Jesus would not have understood, we are very much mistaken. Although he lived much of his life in a largely agrarian environment, it was overlaid by a highly complex religious culture, and overwhelmed by the urbanized, global hegemony of the Roman Empire. His context was more relevant to our present urban predicament than ever we may have imagined.

Visiting Israel/Palestine for the first time we are struck by how very small the place is, and how compact the country in which Jesus undertook his ministry. About 150 years before his birth, the northern territories of Galilee were populated by the Hasmoneans or Maccabees, who built a series of forts to defend their culture from the surrounding gentile kingdoms. Herod the Great who, having received the title King of the Jews from the Roman Senate, had to fight an horrific three-year war against their descendants and others in order to secure his kingdom. He was so frightened of losing his grip on power that he had many executed during those troubles, including the Hasmonean heroine Marianne, so that many rebel families named their daughters Mary, in her memory. Herod then proceeded to undertake the most ambitious building programme of his time. Building in an innovative style which was a mixture of Hasmonean, Hellenic and Roman architectural genres, he created the new world-class port of Sebastos and its adjoining city of Caesarea Maritima, with its palace, theatre, aqueduct and harbour. One cannot but be impressed by this city even when one visits its ruins today. Crossan and Reed say, 'Nothing tells so clearly that Romanization equalled urbanisation equalled commercialisation as the great storehouses and giant break-waters of that all-weather harbour.'[5] In the north of his territories Herod built a temple at Caesarea Philippi, but apart from that, never touched Galilee. That was left to one of his successors, Herod Antipas.

We might say that it was Antipas who brought the Roman Empire, with its intensive urbanization and commercialization, to the home of Jesus. Hoping to secure his hold on the minds of the Jews, he dumped his Nabatean wife and married into the strongly Jewish Hasmonean line. But even this did not win everybody's approval because his new wife was his brother's ex-wife. John the Baptist spoke out against it immediately. The Hasmonean city of Sepphoris, just an hour's walk from Nazareth, had been put down by Varus the Roman legate during their uprising, but Antipas now decided to rebuild it as his own Galilean headquarters. It could well be that on return from Egypt, Jesus' family had been attracted to Nazareth because there would have been plenty of work there for carpenters and builders during the rebuilding of the city. Some even suggest that Jesus' family were themselves originally pro-Hasmonean and perhaps had roots in Sepphoris before its uprising and destruction.[6] When Jesus was about twenty, Antipas decided to link his territories more firmly to the global trade routes by building a brand-new city, named Tiberias in honour of the new Roman emperor, on the banks of the Galilean lake. It was built for the sole purpose of attracting traders across to the western side of the lake, and with the development of a new road link he tied the whole of his Galilean territory into the Empire's network. This certainly put Antipas on the global map but he could not sustain these northern territories through income from trade alone. It was the fertile land which made Galilee such an economic prize, but its fields now came under enormous strain to produce sufficient crops to feed the escalating population and at the same time to produce the tax revenues required to fund Antipas' building and development schemes.

Antipas was taxing at a rate of between 25 and 40 per cent of both income and produce, which forced the farmers to grow less crops for their own sustenance and produce cash crops instead. The resultant problems were similar to those we see today. Many farmers were driven into debt and so lost their strips of land to foreign purchasers, and became instead tenants or day labourers. Galilee became increasingly commercialized, with produce and money being efficiently transferred from the land to the city, and while wealth and luxury increased at one end of society, at the other, people were ground down into increasing poverty. Expensive architecture in the new city meant over-intensive agriculture in the countryside. Jesus knew he would be listened to by the dispossessed peasantry when he proclaimed, 'blessed are you who are destitute, the Kingdom of God is yours'. But while the Kingdom of God might be theirs, it was clear to them that the kingdom of Herod Antipas was not!

Jesus therefore goes out of his way to demonstrate how very different his Kingdom is from that of the Herods. For example, it is instructive that he does not choose to base his ministry in either of Antipas' principal cities, and indeed the Bible includes no reference to him visiting either of them during his missions. The cities were always the means by which Herod and Rome kept control of the villages and farms, and Jesus therefore adopts a radically different style, which has nothing in common with either that of the Roman emperor or Herod. Sepphoris and Tiberias would have supported populations of about 12,000 at the time of Jesus, but instead we read of Jesus establishing his connections with Capernaum, a town of only about 1,000 inhabitants. Even then he does not let it become the headquarters of his work and instead rejoices in the fact that while 'foxes [Herod] have holes and the birds of the air [the Roman eagle] have their nests, the Son of man has nowhere to lay his head' (Luke 9.58).

The cities of Sepphoris and Tiberias, together with the other surrounding Hellenistic towns, housed an increasingly alien aristocracy. They had no ties to the land except that they reaped the benefits of its taxation and exploitation. This was a recipe for disaster in a society which believed that the land had been bequeathed to all the people by their God, as part of their covenant relationship. Social tension and political ferment were bound to be the outcome – Jesus lived at a very tense time. The sacred covenant was therefore interpreted differently by groups who stood to gain from a biased reading of it. The Pharisees saw the Torah Law as binding on all people and pressured even the peasants to keep the Sabbath so strictly that they were increasingly unable to pay their taxes because they were now only able to work the land six days in seven. The Sadducees on the other hand saw the Torah Law as the special preserve of religious professionals like themselves and wanted the power it signified to be centred particularly in Jerusalem and its Temple, where they and their allies presided. So the powerful used the religious culture with its Torah Law as a proof that their power and wealth was a God-given right.

However, just as the pressure of global culture today breeds an antagonistic local response, so also in ancient peasant cultures we learn that a 'shadow culture' would develop in opposition to the culture of the rulers. The American New Testament scholar, William Herzog, believes that is exactly what had been happening in the villages of Galilee, and that Jesus

> interpreted the Torah not as a representative of the great tradition emanating from Jerusalem, but as one who embodied the little tradition found in the villages and countryside of Galilee . . . The far-reaching extent of the debates suggests that, by the first century, the Torah was providing a totalising worldview and orientation. Seen in this context, Jesus' debates about the Torah are more than quibbles over details; they define a struggle over whose worldview will prevail.[7]

If Herzog and his colleagues are interpreting the archaeological, historical and textual evidence correctly, then we begin to build a picture of Jesus as a person who understands only too well the complex power relationships that existed between the urban and rural communities in which he lived. He set out to create his Kingdom community by building on the 'stones' of the covenant tradition that had been rejected by the controllers of the 'great tradition' in Jerusalem. This tradition, which institutionalized religion and made Torah Law oppressive of the poor, emanated especially from the cities and out through their networks of Sadducees, Herodians and Pharisees, whereas the peasants continued to hold to a more liberating reading of the faith – and it was upon this liberating tradition that Jesus built.

Many of Jesus' stories were clearly related to the frightful conditions of the peasantry. He spoke of absentee landlords, of the rich who demanded ever greater harvests, and the fearful urban tax collectors to whom the peasants had to pay their tribute. But just as Jesus did not confine himself to the cities and villages, neither was he confined to the land, for he made his way to the fishing families of the great Galilean lake where he found fishermen ready to give up their trade to follow him. Fishing had largely been undertaken by local farmers who would fish between sowing and harvest when the land did not demand so much of their attention. The fish had been eaten immediately after the catch until the introduction, during the late Hellenistic and Roman period, of new food technologies centred on the salt-packing factories in and around Magdala. The introduction of this technology allowed the global empire to trade salted fish of the finest quality, together with Galilean 'garum', a spicy fish sauce. This trade was of benefit to all – except of course those who now caught the fish at much reduced prices, together with the labourers who fled from the depleted farms and vineyards to work in the salt-packing factories. Fishermen had good reason to be attracted by the revolutionary words of Jesus.

When Jesus established his discipleship group and chose twelve of them to represent the twelve renewed tribes of Israel, it is clear that he was making a bid for the inauguration of an alternative polity. However, in the year of his birth 2,000 rebels had been crucified in Jerusalem in an attempt to put a stop to such revolutionary projects, so Jesus knew that in proclaiming his Kingdom he was courting danger. Jesus certainly did not adopt the tactics of the Zealot Sicarii, the inventors of urban terrorism, who assassinated collaborators amid the jostle of urban crowds, but his proclamation of an alternative Kingdom would nonetheless have incited the fury of Rome, Jerusalem and Tiberias. In spite of this, Jesus launched his ministry just an hour's walk away from Sepphoris, in the village of Nazareth (Luke 4.16f.) by quoting words from Isaiah, which proclaimed that freedom from all oppression would be God's gift with the coming of the year of the Lord's favour. Jesus then announced that, 'This text is being fulfilled today even while you are listening.' No longer need the upstart kingdoms of Rome and the Herods dominate the mind-sets of the people – there was another divine tradition of Kingdom which was now being fulfilled in Jesus.

The challenge of Jesus

Jesus lived in a Galilee where a cultural battle was raging, and he chose to engage in that conflict in order to see God's loving will prevail. With his small mixed group of men and women alongside him, he invited them to live out a new way of being in community in the face of the dominating cultures of hate and greed. He welcomed them into his inclusive, alternative Kingdom community and taught them to engage in critical solidarity alongside those who had been cast aside. He courageously 'set his face to go to Jerusalem' (Luke 9.51, NRSV), the city which had become the very seat of the Roman hegemony which worked through Herod and the corrupted institutional religion of Israel. On his way to the capital city Jesus told his parable stories and enacted sacraments that would shake the city to its foundations. His every local action had global *and universal* significance, and at the heart of his revolutionary message he proclaimed, 'the time has come, the Kingdom of God is close at hand. Repent and believe the Good News'.

7 | The Marks of the Kingdom

Christ the King

As we steep ourselves in the Gospel narratives we come to see that Jesus in many senses *is* the Kingdom, and the Kingdom *is* Jesus. When we belong to the Kingdom we belong to Christ; when we enact his will we acknowledge his Reign; when God's Kingdom comes we see the risen Christ. Yet, throughout the Gospels, Jesus nowhere asks us to call him King – nowhere does he act in the way that worldly monarchs were expected to act. He never forces himself upon us, never seeks to dominate, always opens up the future for us to choose. So it is that the Kingdom comes about, not by way of God's manipulation of our history, but by offering us the story and asking us to become its actors – playing our part in its consummation. Because God leaves us the choice, this means that the Kingdom in our midst is always provisional and not complete – that God's will is not always done on earth. The Kingdom is offered as the fulfilment of God's covenant with us, but we do not always play the part God asks of us.

To help us play our part, Jesus offers us a prayer which is easy to remember and which summarizes the principles of the Kingdom he inaugurates among us. As with every generation before, we must find the meanings of the prayer in our own way and for our own time, and in doing so we will discover how the Lord's Prayer serves as the royal road to the Kingdom. It signposts how we might best live, serve and become what the Kingdom requires, marking out the new culture, the frame of reference, by which we know we belong to Christ. Each phrase of the prayer speaks to us in our contemporary urban predicament and helps us reflect theologically upon it, pointing to the possibilities of the Kingdom in our midst.

Awe and wonder

Our Father, which art in heaven, hallowed be thy name.

In Kingstanding, Birmingham, I became involved in the Lord Mayor's carnival. Our youth club had created a majestic Viking ship and the youngsters had dressed as Nordic warriors and paraded the ship through the streets of the city. That same evening, as if to celebrate their wonderful achievement, the youth club disco thundered on into the night, luckily with no fights, but plenty of high spirits. Two exultant young men pushed through the crowded hall and accosted me. 'Vicar, it's all bin just *awesome!*' I knew then that the club had just been awarded its highest accolade.

One of my greatest delights is exploring a city I've never visited before. I love to gaze upwards at the soaring buildings, to take a side-street and discover something of the hidden city, to admire the brutality or graciousness of the architectural styles, to sit outside a pub and watch the wonderful parade of passers-by. All this gives me such a buzz, taking me beyond myself and leaving me in awe of the dizzy complexity of God's creation. Awesome! Working long-term in urban ministry offers constant opportunity to admire and wonder. We can be stunned, not only by the complexity and vitality of urban life, but also by the humble faithfulness of the poor mother who manages somehow to get her family through the day, or the supportive carefulness of the receptionist dealing with the worries of an elderly enquirer. We can be brought up sharp by the ingratitude of the beggar too, as he draws our attention away from our own superficial generosity to the underlying injustice of his plight. Kofi Annan spoke of the 'squalor amid the splendour', but there is also an abundance of 'splendour amid the squalor', and that can be so moving as to make us recognize that, from time to time, we are balancing on the margins of something quite profound. It is as if we are only touching the very hem of the garment and not the man himself; but even so, it is awesome.

The 'man himself' begins his prayer with the words, 'Our Father, which art in heaven, hallowed be thy name.' He offers us a moment to do as Moses did at the burning bush, and take off our shoes and acknowledge that the ground on which we stand is holy ground. Living the Kingdom starts here and ends here, just as does the prayer, with an acknowledgement of the holiness and the majesty of God our Father who, for all that holiness, comes so close that we glimpse the divine presence in our midst.

In Luke's Gospel, Jesus offers his disciples the Kingdom Prayer just after he has been sitting with Martha and Mary and has helped Martha, 'who was distracted by all the serving', to realize that reflection and contemplation are also essential ingredients of a Kingdom lifestyle. Gazing on Christ in worship is to acknowledge him as our King before anything else of worth can happen.

We begin here, with awe, alongside the wise men from the east bowing at the manger of the Christ child, and learn to perceive beauty in the most unexpected places. With this prayerful attitude at the heart of our Kingdom living, we are better able to honour the beggar at the vicarage door as a child of the same heavenly Father, and seek out his beauty as one of God's children. But beauty is not always clearly apparent on the surface of urban life. Martin Wallace begins one of his *City Prayers*[1] with mention of some familiar sights: 'An old mattress has been dumped at the end of my road: an eyesore for all. Around the corner a mangled car seat is wedged dangerously high on the barbed wire, above the broken wooden fence, under the railway arch.' Martin Luther was fond of pointing out that it was important to adorn our church buildings because the poor live with ugliness, and they should be allowed to experience something of God's beauty – they need art as much as bread, he suggested. There are beautiful things to be seen in our cities – and just sometimes we are moved to agree that 'earth hath not anything to show more fair' than the Thames at Westminster – but usually it takes the eye of the contemplative spirit to see under the skin of a poor urban situation and acknowledge the beauty that God has placed there. The Christian does well to seek out the urban poets, photographers and artists who are there in abundance, whose skill with their chosen medium may sometimes be a little primitive, but their inner eye is so often a gift to the community.

Nevertheless, despite moments of beauty, there will inevitably be another old mattress at the corner of the next street. Our lives are messy, the street is dirty and the community lets itself down. Even when we try, we find ourselves fighting against the odds. The local authority decided to plant trees along the North Circular Road recently in order to create a healthier environment for London people, only to find that all the trees died because of the intensity of the traffic pollution. Things have become very bad.

The prophets record that when initially receiving their call they found themselves humbled and fearful in the presence of the Holy God, but this in turn helped them to realize how important the message was that they had received. Martin Luther King Jr proclaimed in his moving sermon that he had 'been to the mountain top' and could therefore return with new vision, determination and strength, to continue his fight for justice in an ugly world. When we stand in awe before the Holy One in our prayer and worship, we find ourselves presented with a judgement upon our own failings and the inadequacies of our society – but then a sense of forgiveness turns that judgement into a vision of what might be. So this initiating sense of awe, with which all Kingdom theology and activity must begin, leads us through judgement and on inevitably to repentance – a change of heart and mind. So we pray, 'Thy will be done.'

Thy will be done: living repentance

Thy Kingdom come, thy will be done, on earth as it is in heaven.

The final chapters of this book will look specifically at some practical outcomes for urban ministry and mission, but we should not race to that practical action without seeking always to link that action with a proper discernment of what God's will is for our urban world and its communities. As we read the city, we can become convinced that there are 'powers and principalities' at work which are seeking to obscure the Kingdom vision, and so we must therefore tear away those obscuring curtains by praying for wisdom and discernment so that we can keep true to the vision.

There is, for example, an obscuring assumption in the public mind that within our urban communities there is a large and persistent core of poor people, and that they pass their deprivation on from one generation to the next. The hidden implication is that their poverty derives from their own family failings. Research proves however[2] that most poor people move through phases of dependency, and most extreme poverty is temporary. There is always the exception, but to think of a huge core of persistently impoverished people is not consistent with the evidence – different people move in and out of extreme poverty at different times, and if they get to that point most work very hard to find ways out of that fearful condition. The same research has shown too that, again contrary to the myth, our welfare state provision of services is not costly in comparative terms, and certainly the stories of abuse of those services are exaggerated to the point of fantasy. Yet on the basis of these blinkered misconceptions, governments continue to shape their policies and mission strategies.

Globalization expects us to 'buy into' its obscuring myths, so, as we pray for God's will to be done, we must make sure that these myths do not succeed in obscuring the Kingdom vision. Let us examine three examples.

1. Commodification

A commodity is something bought and sold in the marketplace for a price. And in our culture everything, including our education, health and housing, seems to be determined not so much by its social value as by its price. We are becoming accustomed to seeing people costed too – costed in and costed out. In the book of Revelation, chapter 13, we read that the mark 666 was placed upon the forehead of citizens for only one reason, and I quote – it 'made it illegal for anyone to buy or sell anything unless he had been branded with the name of the beast or with its number' (v. 17, NJB). The New Testament clearly states that 666 is about the marketplace, where everyone is given a price-tag, brand and label, but not necessarily their value.

It is therefore very interesting that the Greek word the New Testament chooses to use for 'Church', *ecclesia*, was the word used in antiquity for an assembly in the marketplace at which the whole community would decide together upon community issues. The Church *ecclesia* was to be an alternative, non-commodifying way of being in the marketplace. Kingdom of God theology must therefore demythologize the market so that it does not become the hidden assumption underlying our life choices, but is only allowed to play its proper part as a helpful and legitimate tool for some of our transactions – and no more.

2. Efficiency

Everyday urban life rushes by on a '24/7' basis, making work into little more than a rat-race. Our Christian traditions hold in very high regard the careful stewardship of our creative gifts and God-given resources, and that promises well for efficiency – but to take that to the extreme of a relentless driven-ness and a heavy-handed exploitation of workers and the world's resources has no warrant in scripture. The Genesis story of creation pictures God as the worker, working each day and pausing each evening to survey the results of the divine creativity, happy to see that it is good, and thus blessing to us the value of productivity, sabbatical rest and relaxation. The gardener who only gardens and never stops to look at the beauty of the garden has somehow missed out on the very reason for gardening. The demand for ever-increasing efficiency in our urban life means that anyone who is not ruthlessly efficient goes to the wall. How different this global drive for competitive efficiency is from the Bible's suggestion that there is a hidden value even in weakness. The prayer to see God's will done on earth as it is in heaven will teach us not to allow competitive efficiency to drive the weak to the wall.

3. Information

Like the Tower of Babel, today's global city prides itself particularly on its information culture. At the press of a button we are in touch with vast reams of data to the extent that many of us now feel we have information overload. The happiest key on the keypad seems to be the delete button. The cultural assumption is, 'The more information I have, the better my judgements will be. If I know this fact or believe that information, then I can assert that I have the truth.' But truth as information was actually the rampant heresy of Gnosticism which assailed the Church in its earliest years and which the Bible vigorously challenged. In the Bible, the word 'to know' does not refer to information at all but to loving intimacy. The God of truth is found in loving relationship and, what is more, actually *is* a relationship – the Holy Trinity. Christian truth is therefore not a statement but a relationship, and it is the quality of the relationship which we have with God through Christ that will be for us the truth (John 15). Information, of course, is a wonderful gift, but if the dominating culture of globalization seeks to make us think that information is the root of all wisdom, then we are being profoundly misled.

The three myths of commodification, efficiency and information may well blind our Kingdom vision, but even the very word 'globalization' itself may hinder our discernment of God's will. Some national governments and local authorities have failed to address injustices which were within their field of responsibility, claiming as an excuse that their hands were tied by global forces. All these myths can so easily blinker our Kingdom vision. We have spoken of commodification, efficiency and information, but we could add privatization, transparency, the market, and many more. Our problem is that these myths often hide behind the most exciting and enjoyable parts of urban culture, such as the media, music production, the arts, professional football and entertainment. From time to time we may hear the complaint that 'money is ruining the game', or 'they're buying artwork only for investment' – but somehow we let the myths continue to define us and our world, and forget to go to the mountain top and renew our Kingdom vision. If we are to work to see the Father's will 'done on earth as in heaven', then we must rise above the idols of earth and 'seek first the Kingdom of God and its righteousness'.

Being good stewards of creation

Give us this day our daily bread.

Bread is the staff of life. It is security and sustenance at its most basic and physical level. And the Kingdom prayer asks that we may have it and share it.

Christians believe that God created matter and therefore values the physical – in God's eyes, matter matters. The Christian creeds affirm belief in the physical resurrection of the body – a doctrine which provides a very strong mandate for us to treat our physicality with immense respect. We are not disembodied spirits, even though intellectual and class élitism has, since the time of Plato, valued mind above matter in the most exploitative ways. In today's urbanized world however, many are made to live their sedentary lives so much by the application of their intellect that they get almost no physical exercise. Watching one screen all day and another each evening is to live life as an 'out of the body' experience.

Away from the desk, however, it's all very different. Urban streets are very physical places[3] – witness the vibrant lights, strident symbols and brash sexuality of the city at night. Every day the city environment bustles and struggles with physical abundance. Here, immense wealth is created, goods in vast tonnage are transported, millions ride the tram or Underground, new office buildings soar into the skies. Here is abundance, but usually exploited only for the advantage of the few. The built environment can be justly shared if it is properly controlled by planners, who should see their work as a means of stewarding the resources of the built urban environment, working in close collaboration with those whom they serve. Urban spaces have often been brutalized in the past and we have inherited the misdemeanours of our forebears. Our white concrete tower blocks with stinking lifts and dangerous stairwells are not the outcome of a governance and political stewardship which has taken seriously the importance of building sustainable human settlements. As for waste, England now sports 45,000 hectares of contaminated and derelict land and just under a million empty buildings.[4] How can we pray, 'Give us this day our daily bread' when we have so evidently squandered our bread from yesterday?

Often one part of the city has lived at the expense of another, the captains of industry allowing whole swathes of the inner city and outer estates, where their workers have lived, to become depressed and desolate.

While heaping our daily bread upon one community, we have wasted the potential of others by offering them sparse and inadequate training, education and opportunity – and such extreme disparity easily leads to social de-stabilization and urban violence. There is abundance in God's creation, and wealth creation in our cities can be beautiful, but never should it be at the expense of the planet or of others – Christ's body has been scourged enough.

Since God is the creator of all things, we could say God is the 'wealth creator' *par excellence*, and the incarnation the bringer of 'added value' to creation by allowing matter to find its true purpose and pleasure in God. We should celebrate the fact that we can share in this creative potential, bringing added value by transformation of material resources and the application of intellectual skill. We should be proud of our workers and the wealth they help to create. We must develop a spirited theology of work and the workplace,[5] to enable lay people to reflect on their working lives with that theology to guide and inspire.

Our economic theory and practice is predicated upon scarcity – that is why we draw economic charts of demand and supply. But God's economy, much to our surprise, is predicated upon generous over-abundance and extraordinary preparedness to share. Labourers in the vineyard are paid a generous day's wage even though they have not been able to work a full day – and 'how much more will the heavenly father give to those who ask him'. Unlike ours, God's economy is one of extravagant generosity. And when it comes to debt, in God's economy it is all forgiveness – even 'seventy times seven times'. This is so different from the loan-shark mentality of our housing estates and our city finance houses. The parables of the Kingdom speak of a glorious liberality of grace as the essence of God's economy – not obligation, nor scarcity, but generosity.

Generosity and even exuberance can often be the gift our young people bring us. Modern dance-club culture offers our urban youngsters a wonderful way to be together. Sophisticated lighting, a pulsating beat, and the charisma of the DJ are accompanied by the creativity of record-scratching, disc-mixing and the poetry of rap. Each dancing young person can express his or her own vitality in a very physical way, while the pounding beat brings all on the dance-floor into a sense of unity – a sense of belonging to the whole as the volume builds and everyone moves together with the rhythm. Our city and town centres come alive each night with thousands of young people thronging together to feel that physical exhilaration and to have fun. They dress in the latest street fashions and make lots of noise, as only young people can. It is good to see this bold confidence in the body being expressed in clubs, pubs and on the street. It has always been a facet of British working-class culture to dress up and express oneself in this physically brash manner, and even today, when I go to an East End party, the sparkle of my bishop's ring pales into insignificance alongside the jewellery that other men and women are wearing.

But for all this outward show of bodily self-confidence, the urban scene is also full of human bodies that have been subjected to disease and malnutrition, poor lifestyles and brutality. We pray for our daily bread because the 'urban deficit' still bites hard into the health, longevity and well-being of the people. Diseases due to poor and dangerous working conditions, together with new and returning diseases like AIDS and TB, hit those who are already vulnerable to financial hardship and poor housing conditions. Arriving at Whitechapel Underground station to visit the London Hospital, one has first to push through the press of alcoholic and drug-dependent homeless people who crowd the station entrance. In poor areas high streets are littered with fast-food outlets which do little to bring the bread of physical nourishment to the locals, and it shows. Their physical condition almost mirrors the disrepair of their surrounding urban environment. Jesus tells a story which promises that the glorious and qualitative banquet of the Kingdom will be shared by all. The stewards are sent out into the poorest quarters of society to compel the outcast to come and share, and only those who have excluded themselves miss out. I believe that there is growing up in the public mind an anger at the exclusion of the poor from the world's banquet. To bring in the Kingdom, our life together must mirror the self-sacrifice which Jesus makes as he forgives us, includes us at the banquet, and gives himself as the bread for the world.

As we forgive: knowing the other

> *And forgive us our trespasses, as we forgive those who trespass against us.*

As a boy, I used to help my grandmother run her jewellery stall in East Ham market. I was not expected to engage in much retail since very little was sold, but I do remember the interminable cups of strong tea over which market traders and shoppers would gather to share the news of the day. Today we use this homely phrase, 'marketplace', to refer to the cut and thrust of international finance and competitive dealing, where it is rare that anyone meets face to face, or knows, or even wants to know, anything at all about the person that they are doing business with. In East Ham market, if you sold a faulty pair of earrings one day you could expect salt in your tea tomorrow, but in today's so-called 'marketplace' you may take your trade to another shop without realizing that the same company owns that store too.

The Lord's Prayer paints a picture of a Kingdom where we have a sense of responsibility one for another. We remember that God is 'Our Father', making us all brothers and sisters in the commonality of the human race. And yet we harbour fear and anxiety on the bus when the only spare seat is next to someone who is dressed in clothes from another culture, and who looks so very different from us. We sense that we have no common language with which to communicate, and all that seems to be communicated is otherness.

The ultimate otherness of God, the profound holiness and mystery of the divine, is even more frightening, so we construct defences against that too – defences of indifference, or more subtly, religiosity – so that God's otherness does not overwhelm us. But the Holy Other God reaches down to us and embraces us intimately, as 'the dear Lord enters in' through the incarnation of our Lord Christ. With God, otherness is no longer the dark alley to exclusion but the open road to reconciled embrace.

Jesus lives the Kingdom by crossing the boundaries of otherness – crossing the ultimate boundary from divinity to humanity, so that the veil of the Temple is torn in two – the holy and the common at last in 'holy communion'. In a land of exclusion and racial conflict, he reaches out even to the collaborator Zacchaeus allowing him to entertain him in his home; the Syro-Phoenician woman, a person of altogether another ethnicity, is granted her request; excluded lepers are healed and welcomed in. Jesus welcomes them, and even brings together into his closest ring of disciples people like Levi the tax collector and Simon the Zealot, who in other circumstances would have been mortal enemies. Jesus' life demonstrates that the Kingdom of God is marked by a welcoming inclusion and embrace of difference and otherness.

That we should be forgiven even as we forgive is a very challenging prospect. It is to reach out for a togetherness in the midst of otherness, a unity in diversity – and that, no one finds easy. In 1991 a somewhat secret meeting took place, headed by the notorious Slobodan Milosevic, which decided to obliterate the city of Sarajevo. The cities have increasingly become places where differences are accepted and communities reconciled; and Sarajevo had been, since medieval times, a great symbol of that cosmopolitan spirit. Those, like Milosevic, who stand for exclusivity and separation, have therefore been hitting out violently at the cosmopolitan cities,[6] raising terror and destruction in the name of separation and religious 'purity'. God's work of reconciliation meets very powerful counter-forces – that our sins may be mutually forgiven must be our ardent prayer.

Reconciliation with the 'enemy'

In vicarage gardens across east London there are still some very old mulberry trees which were planted to welcome the Huguenot silk weavers when they fled from Europe to make their homes in the Protestant cities of England. The migratory process has continued down the years to such an extent that a visitor from outside the city may be very surprised indeed to encounter the amazing mix of cultures and styles which is east London today. The accelerating processes of globalization have made investment capital more mobile than ever before, and while inflowing capital is sometimes over-valued by the host community, the migrant labour and skill which follows that capital is very often under-valued or even despised.

Migration is at the very heart of the biblical narrative, from Abraham, through Moses and the Exile, to Jesus and the early Church. Many governments around the world however are colluding with the media in presenting the refugees not as modern equivalents of the Holy Family in exile, but as a 'bogus' strain upon the receiving economy, and this take on the situation is being accepted even by many intelligent people. Recently, in a local policy think-tank, I was asked by government executives to name a social issue of consequence for our region. I suggested 'racism', but was shocked to hear their response: 'Ah, yes, those asylum-seekers.' Any person of colour was still, in their view, someone other – other than British, other than friend, other than themselves.

In this climate, some ethnic minority communities which have been in Britain for many years have felt so stigmatized that they have welcomed the mutual support and solace to be found in remaining together in ethnic enclaves – some choosing this lifestyle as a preferred option, others being forced and bullied into it. With separated schooling, shopping, leisure and religious observance, this has produced a series of parallel communities, who may live side by side, but who never have a chance to meet. In 2001 the eruption of alienated communities on the streets of Oldham, Burnley and Bradford highlighted the need for the government to address these divisions, and the resultant Cantle Report[7] described these parallel but alienated communities as in need of issue-based investment and long-term support for the development of community cohesion.

We sense fragmentation too, in the workplace. Most of the unions have been carefully disabled by governments through the years, and the workplace has been informalized and restructured in many ways. Women, prepared to work part-time hours, have been used to undermine the men's hold on full-time posts so that the sense of togetherness and solidarity has been greatly diminished.

Further fragmentation of once cohesive communities can be brought about by removing a vulnerable group's language. Not long ago poorer segments of the British population could refer to themselves as 'working class' and thereby have a sense of themselves as a somewhat distinctive group within society. Very steadily however, talk of 'working class' and any kindred terms have been expunged from common discourse, making it difficult for them to retain a sense of belonging and solidarity, and so they are more easily manipulated and targeted. The same fragmentation is encouraged by the terms 'social exclusion' and 'inclusion' – the word 'poor' having been dropped entirely. This neatly bypasses issues of power, and puts the onus on the poor to get *themselves* into the marketplace and reduce their own 'exclusion'. It is a language game that rarely asks us who the social 'excluders' are, or how they can be made to stop their excluding and divisive behaviour.

These processes, which fragment what were once close communities, run counter to the grain of a gospel which so evidently respects our identities and wants us to meet face to face, openly and honestly. The Lord's Prayer for mutual forgiveness looks to a Kingdom where these language games that oppressive cultures play, as they try to keep us from knowing one another in solidarity, will be dispelled so that we will at last know even as we are known. Even on the cross, where Jesus is attacked by the powers of fragmentation and dislocation, he prays, 'Father, forgive them – they do not know what they are doing.'

In the Genesis story, the arrogant builders of the Tower of Babel are scattered abroad. Their language is confused and they become alienated from one another in a fragmented world. At Pentecost on the other hand, the Holy Spirit brings reconciliation, and pilgrims who are gathered in Jerusalem from all around the globe hear the same Good News each in their own language. Each language, each separate culture, is individually respected, and yet at the same time the Good News unites them.

Our gospel must become, like Pentecost, 'multi-voiced', allowing the Holy Spirit to speak in each language and in each culture and context in ways that each of us will understand – the gospel in a local accent.[8] Many voices will then issue from those experiences of encounter with God around the world; and although different, the voices when brought together in the Kingdom will create a harmony of song. As the full choir sings, so the catholic truth (that is, that which 'accords with the whole' – *kata holon*) will be heard by the whole Christian community. In this way those who are 'other' become included, and we begin to sense something of the power of the prayer, 'forgive us as we are forgiven'. It implies a mutual respect and acceptance which is life-transforming.

When thousands gathered in Coventry to celebrate the tenth anniversary of the Church Urban Fund, young people from Nottingham presented a challenging drama which called on the Church to respect young adults as persons through whom the Spirit can speak – but who are so often demonized and alienated. They shouted across the cathedral, 'If you treat us like rubbish, we'll behave like rubbish!' Some people feel so atomized and hassled by the aggressive and polarizing experience of today's culture that they become fearful even for their own personal cohesion. Amid all the fragmentation of urban life it is easy to lose all memory of who we truly are – and as our own identity feels threatened so we hit out at those who appear to have found a sense of identity by belonging to an alternative group. The person who looks vaguely different begins to count more and more as an enemy. Yet, the good news is that it can be precisely this tearing apart – this fragmentation – which can bring us back to a sense of who we are. The priest takes the bread, and giving thanks, breaks it into fragments and shares it out, and through this process it becomes the one Body of Christ. To give life, Jesus is himself torn into pieces in the Eucharist, but says, 'do this *in remembrance* of me'. To remember who we are, we have to own up to our fragmentation. When this is done we can listen to one another's stories, not fearfully wanting to prove to others that we are more 'together' than they are, and that our story is the only true one, but welcoming each story, knowing that we are all but fragments of the whole. And until we learn to do this together we remain lost in the miscommunication and polarization about which the Tower of Babel story warns.

The urban Church must be a reconciling, listening and forgiving community. In Poplar we were always aware that all around us were homeless people on the streets – but the inclination was to keep ourselves to ourselves rather than meet them and hear their voice. Our youth group were not content with that separated existence and so determined that one evening we would all go together to the local gathering points for homeless people and learn from them there. We took food, drink and blankets, but our main purpose was to meet and listen. The youngsters came back full of new wisdom. That week they prepared a dramatic presentation for us which they staged on Sunday evening during the worship service. Connections were made, the voices were heard, the stories told, and parallel tracks at last met together, just for a moment.

It has always fascinated me that, although the Exodus theme is a key motif of the Hebrew scriptures, it was not the model taken up by Jesus or the early Church. Exodus is not the best story for Jesus, for Jesus is not advocating escape – quite the reverse. Jesus eats the Passover meal as his Last Supper with his friends, but then he does *not* escape. On the contrary, Jesus teaches his disciples that they will find their freedom, their identity and their salvation in engagement. A loving relationship even with the so-called 'enemy' is the essential and astonishing demand of the Kingdom message. Jesus therefore tells his disciples to 'stay in the city', to confront the urban challenges, not flee from them into a holy huddle. It is there that we too will meet God in the midst of the struggle, surrounded by others who are very different, so that we can learn to let our sins be forgiven 'as we forgive those who sin against us', and so experience God's Kingdom gift of reconciliation.

Deliver us from evil: structural sin

Lead us not into temptation, but deliver us from evil.

Walk any urban street and consider the complex logistics which make it function. Much of it is hidden from view. There are all the underground water and electrical connections for each household, and the web of relationships between families, shopkeepers, employers, office workers and friends. In addition there are the more distant structures of management which supervise the road cleaning, the sewerage systems, the educational and health services. The civic life of local politics and the national and regional systems of governance all play their part too in what we initially observed as a simple street in an urban district. In today's globalized world, we must also take into account the powerfully combined forces of technology, politics and economics – all working dynamically together to impose their structures upon urban regions and the life of each street and each human being within it. So we readily acknowledge that the urban scene is not merely the sum of all the human beings who live there, but consists of so much more – and if we do not take account of this 'so much more', then our urban ministry can only be partial and severely limited. Even today some church ministers see their role as caring only for the households of the parish, without giving a thought to the institutions, the economy, employment and commerce, which are also key to the area and people they serve.

In *Power to the Powerless*, I tell the story of a small group of Christians who set about doing theology in the back streets of the city of Birmingham. As they looked carefully together at the issues and problems of the area it became plain to them that they were encountering much more than simply the faults and shortcomings of the individual officers who were failing to serve the community or behaving badly within it. They were up against structural sin – faults and failings in the underlying systems which affected the locality very deeply. But this was not an easy concept to handle.

Recently, the Essex Race Relations Council asked me to define 'institutional racism', a term which had caused arguments when it was used in the Stephen Lawrence Report. The Report said that the way in which the racist crime against Stephen had been investigated led them to think there was structural or institutional racism within the police force. Many were angry and replied, 'Perhaps there are a few rotten apples in the barrel, but not many.' However, when the phrase 'institutional racism' is used, I take it to mean that even if there were no rotten apples in the barrel at all, the fault is that the barrel is racist. The structures which surround us have a way of controlling us – they form the culture which we must critique.

The Birmingham group was an intentionally Christian group who were minded to act in accordance with the Kingdom of God frame of reference and so they naturally turned to the Bible to help discern a way forward. It was when they turned to the book of Revelation that they found pictures and symbols which gave them a handle on the nature of structures, and moved them forward into action. St John is imprisoned, a captive in the Roman penal colony on Patmos Island, and writes a cryptic letter, the book of Revelation, describing his vision. He writes of a victorious battle in heaven, and an ongoing battle on earth. He sees a harlot, who represents the compromising ambiguities of the city of Rome, and a beast, called forth by the devil. The Beast's followers make inhuman demands upon the people and in chapter 13 they all have to chant adoringly, 'Who can compare with the Beast; who can fight against him?' Individuals within the empire are powerless unless they succumb to its requirements, internalize its demands and make them their own – everyone has to wear the mark of the Beast.

When we pray, 'deliver us from evil', we are being reminded that the complex hidden structures of society are not always benign, but can be quite beastly. I can be moved on from one department to another, and meet wonderfully supportive people in each department, but while I go round and round the system I may still never find an answer to my housing problem. I find myself battling not against any of the individuals I meet along the way, but against some beastly undercurrent which has us all in its web of muddle and mystification. Forms, categories and procedures, all produced by well-meaning officers, all lead back to the same conclusion – all of us together feel powerless to sort out the problem. St John, imprisoned on Patmos, knew the benefits of living in a Roman Empire which had brought order, trade and leadership to the world. But the poor had experienced that same order, trade and leadership as control, exploitation and subservience. The imperial culture was the Beast which had infiltrated every avenue of life, until its domination led people to believe, 'there is no alternative'.

The Beast often makes us feel impotent because of the sheer scale of the problems. Ray Bakke tells of a certain Chicago hospital where as many as 46 per cent of the births are now HIV positive, crack-cocaine addicted or alcohol damaged – the Beast is just too vast to manage. We know that in the schools of our own country the number of GCSE passes attained by our pupils is in inverse proportion to the number who qualify for free school meals.[9] There is clearly some sort of relationship here, but it is so complex that we feel it has us beaten. More often than not, council officials and elected members know full well that the systems need changing and do their best to improve them, but are frustrated by lack of success. One housing officer, having to implement a cut-back in provision on an inner-city housing estate, was despairing at the fact that the tenants had taken it all lying down. 'If only they would be more angry, I'd feel better.'

As I grew up, I distinctly had the feeling that in the East End, the alternative economy was so well networked that, as Woody Allen put it, original sin meant purchasing anything retail. You were thought both unimaginative and not a participating member of the community if you spurned the network. If something 'fell off the back of a lorry' we could see no harm in it, just as some urban developers today see no harm working the structures of regeneration to their own advantage. I remember being so angry having to wait in a cold hall with a shivering group of local people until the developer turned up with his consultant in a felt-collared coat and BMW. He was a nice enough man, but a system which allowed this disparity just did not seem right to me.

Some structures promise well, but then let us down. Those who served in urban ministry for many years thought that the change in the political climate to a partnership culture might have presaged the dawn of a new age. However, whereas in the past the Church felt able to engage issues and areas where other organizations were unable to reach, and ran all sorts of alternative and imaginative schemes, today we are very limited in what we are allowed to do. We can find ourselves overwhelmed by the bureaucracy of our partners. Government partnerships demand that we determine outcomes or 'outputs' even before the project begins – so stifling the imaginative and adventurous flare of former times. Their very understandable need to hold everyone financially accountable has led to a culture of paperwork and self-protection, while the complexities of their programmes has everyone baffled. A clergyman who was seconded to a government department to ease communication between the Church's urban mission and the government's urban policy tells me that it took him at least six months of strenuous study before he could discern how the government systems were supposed to work.

The urban congregation will do well to pray, 'deliver us from evil', for they face dangers, wickedness and evil, not only in the corridors of bureaucracy but moment by moment on the street, in the pub, or at the hands of their neighbours. One night I was called out by the owner of the local Chinese take-away who had noticed smoke billowing from the church windows. I rushed across the road to find that Charlie, a well-known local addict, was intent on setting the whole church alight. The fire brigade managed to limit the damage, but Charlie was arrested on the spot and sent to prison. When I asked him the next day why on earth he'd tried to set fire to the church, he told me that at the time he thought it would be a nice thing to do. Charlie was a lovable character who had started sniffing glue as a child, and had lived for years in the stair-well of the block of flats where his family were tenants. Anyone who knew the full story was aware that it was not a simple matter of blaming Charlie for the fire – but to say exactly where blame did lie was beyond me. Similarly, some years later my wife was threatened by a young couple with whom she had been working. Their life together was a mixture of domestic violence, theft and addiction. They were eventually arrested for attempting to murder a shop owner, simply because he had refused to open his shop after midnight to serve them. People who live their lives as near to the edge as this seem to have lost any reference points at all by which they might seek to live a pleasant or moral life. How earnestly both we and they need to pray, 'deliver us from evil'.

Jesus makes himself extremely vulnerable to the powers of evil by journeying to Jerusalem to confront the urban élites who control and constrain the populace. He is crucified by those powers, nailed to the cross, and from that 'vantage point' he stares out across a city caught in the web of evil structures and human temptation. Jesus was right to weep for the city and now, as he hangs on the cross, he shares the betrayal, the degradation, the vulnerability and the marginalization of its urban poor.

But on the cross Jesus also displays the mysterious power which God gives to those who do his will. The tiny project offered by the small inner-city congregation can be a life-giving gift to those who are touched by it. The courageous witness of a few housing-estate Christians can change evil policies if offered in the power of weakness, for such action participates in the power of the crucifixion to save. 'What is sown is perishable, but what is raised is imperishable; what is sown is contemptible but what is raised is glorious; what is sown is weak, but what is raised is powerful' (1 Corinthians 15.43).

Thine is the Kingdom: structural righteousness

For thine is the Kingdom, the Power and the Glory.

Those who look on from a distance may be so aware of evil in our towns, cities and estates that they become blind to the presence of God's delight and righteousness there too. In recent decades significant books have been written about the powers and principalities of evil, but it is also important for us to acknowledge that Christ's death and resurrection have transformed the world for good.

In the book of Revelation the people despaired that none could fight against the Beast, but John's vision goes on to disclose that the one who is able to conquer the Beast and open the future to righteousness is a sacrificial Lamb – the Lamb of God. The Lamb displays such vulnerability and self-sacrificial daring that the powers of evil are overcome and all the company of heaven rejoices.

The biblical tradition is clear that the structures of a society are not inevitably and irrevocably evil. They are in fact necessary to the proper ordering and management of any society – and in that sense are a divine gift. The writer of the letter to the Colossians declares that, in Jesus 'were created all things in heaven and on earth – all things were created through him and for him. He exists before all things and in him all things hold together' (Colossians 1.16–18). In this passage, the word we translate as 'hold together' is the Greek word from which we derive our word 'systematize'. So the Bible acknowledges that the systems and structures that surround us are not there by mistake, but exist to give creation an ordered pattern of life and possibility. St Paul therefore acknowledges that even the *Torah*-Law, which had given him so much trouble, was nevertheless right and good for those born under it (Romans 7.12). Without some form of law, marketplace, education, systems of house building, and so on, no human society would prove sustainable. Science itself is founded upon the faith that some ordered pattern must at some level always be discernible in everything around us. The Bible shows us that the structures are indeed there to be of service, but they have fallen from grace. The letter to the Colossians goes on to tell how Jesus has therefore thrown the spotlight on to them – stripping and unmasking them for what they are – and in his crucifixion, has made a public spectacle of them by placarding their evil for all to see. The Romans were fond of their triumphant processions into the city after a great victory when the vanquished would be paraded in chains. So the letter to the Colossians says that Jesus 'has stripped the sovereignties and the ruling forces, and paraded them in public, behind him in his triumphal procession' (Colossians 2.15, NJB). The Lamb has triumphed over the Beast, allowing the structures of society still to function, but now fully stripped of their mythology, and back in their proper place in the order of creation – at the back of the procession, there to serve.

With this Kingdom frame of mind, we can appreciate the structure we call 'the market', but refuse to let it dominate us. The market has proved itself in many ways, but it has also shown us that it needs virtue to control it – or it will get the upper hand and walk at the front of the procession. That is why we rely upon accountants to monitor companies rather than rely upon the 'invisible hand' of the market to dominate the outcomes – and in the light of contemporary scandals, this is also why we have learnt to monitor the accountants!

The Revelation of St John declares that in the final analysis God triumphs over the evils of society, but in this interim time, Christians must engage in what the Quakers referred to as the 'War of the Lamb', bearing on our foreheads no longer the brand of the Beast, but the baptismal mark of the Lamb. We must engage the powers of evil, just as did the Lamb, with courageous action and vulnerability. Soon after I moved from the parish of Poplar, I learnt from Nick Holtam, Vicar of the next-door parish on the Isle of Dogs, that a fascist named Derek Beackon had been elected as the local councillor. One of Nick's congregation wrote, 'I spent four years of my life fighting Nazis, and now we've voted them in!' The local congregations met together and decided to set up a campaign structured around the principles of letting the truth be told, of building bridges, increasing the electoral turn-out, and helping to strengthen the local democratic parties in readiness for the next election. The Churches had people all around the community wearing specially made rainbow ribbons, and the very carefully crafted campaign soon won the support of hundreds of local people. The exercise proved successful in many ways. First, the fascists were overwhelmingly defeated at the voting booth, but it also led the Churches to continue building bridges, addressing concerns about housing, employment, cultural differences and so on. It is difficult to think of any organization other than the Church that would have had the necessary presence across the communities, the vision and courage to address the political structures, and the ability to mobilize so many people and groups. The structures of society are there to serve, but sometimes in the War of the Lamb they have to be unmasked and made to serve to the glory of God, and accord with their original purpose.

It would have been easier for the New Testament Church to have denied the inclusivity of Pentecost, just as it would have been easier for the Christians on the Isle of Dogs to have let the local election go unchallenged. But prayer prompts in us a deep realization that holding all together is the Triune God, who forever brings beauty out of ugliness, form out of meaninglessness and binds us together across the barriers which try to separate us. In the famous Russian icon painted by Andrei Rublev, we see three figures, seemingly representing the persons of the Holy Trinity. They are seated at a meal which they bless by their presence, and to which they appear graciously to invite us as we look on in wonder at their elegance and dignity. The three figures are guests at a banquet and, as they offer to share their meal with us, so the icon breathes into us an awareness of how fallen structures can be redeemed in righteousness. For all their calm and tranquillity, it is as if the figures are, so to speak, dancing one with another. Each one is different from the others – a person in his or her own right – but each is nothing without the others in the dance. It is a gracious interweaving of the three persons, Father, Son and Holy Spirit, as they care for one another, but always inclusive of ourselves as we look on in wonder and awe. It is a picture of the Kingdom of God – of structures redeemed – a picture which we long to see rewritten across creation as we pray, 'thine is the Kingdom, the Power and the Glory'.

For ever and ever: the apostolic mission

For ever and ever, Amen.

The Lord's Prayer ends with a glorious acclamation of triumphant hope and a commitment to God's future. For just as the Kingdom is now and 'not yet', so also our present mission must always be undertaken with an eye on what, by God's grace, may yet come to be. Our little mustard seed projects have a way of opening up to God's greater possibilities.

Just a short distance from where I now live is one of the most deprived areas in the UK. Hidden away in the heart of the community, a little tin tabernacle is home to a small but committed congregation of Christians who have opened their buildings and their hearts to local youngsters. Each year Jill Edwards encourages her little group to think beyond the boundaries of their community. One year they responded to the challenge by raising money to send to the street children of Calcutta, and followed that the next with a small gift to the children of Kirinyaga in Kenya. They did not expect to receive in reply a letter of thanks telling them how much the gift meant to the Kenyan people and that they had used the money to lay the foundations of a church centre in their village. From then on it was not possible to hold the Thames-side youngsters back. They roped in everybody they could think of and over a period of years produced enough to complete the African building in fine style – and certainly a lot grander than the tin tabernacle in their own parish. The project has stimulated not only a long-term relationship between Kirinyaga and the home parish, bringing children and adults together across the globe, but has prompted Maureen Ivin, another of the clergy team, to become a formidable campaigner for international fair trade and children's rights. All who hear about the project are humbled by the generous energy of the young people, the learning that it has all generated and the long-term commitment of this tiny congregation to be a sign of the Kingdom in a poor community so much in need of some good news.

The Church is the privileged instrument of the Kingdom of God, but is sometimes more concerned for its own welfare than it is to sacrifice itself for the sake of the Kingdom. The Church of England is still thought by some urban communities to be 'them what think they're coming to do us good and turn us all middle class like them'. The reality may be very different, but people's expectations of us can be very low. Others may not welcome our coming because, especially since 11 September 2001, 'religion' is seen to be simply a bad and dangerous thing. Polly Toynbee, writing in the *Guardian*, put it bluntly: 'Religion isn't nice. It kills!' People of faith may unfairly be assumed to have closed minds and to be violent towards those with whom they disagree. All this means that when we talk about 'new ways of being Church', a phrase which has gained much acclaim of late, rather than interpret it to mean thinking about fresh ways of attracting people to more of the same, we really must stress the need to be a changed community. The Church must change radically into a more listening, engaging and trustworthy community, and must be seen to have become so.

On a Coventry housing estate a group of young mums from the church decided that the children of the playgroup would do well to have somewhere safe to play in the open air rather than to remain always in the church hall. Outside the church was a patch of scrubby ground, so one Saturday they tried to make something of it. A gang of young lads began to abuse the women, telling the mums better ways to go about the work. But the youngsters were surprised to receive an open invitation to help and, as Saturdays passed, they themselves became committed to the ground-clearing. Trust and friendship grew up and all sorts of imaginative ideas came to fruition. A clown day created even more local interest and eventually the little church found it had an exciting community project on its hands. They have become convinced that evangelism is about sharing the good news of trust, hope and reconciliation between the different generations on their estate. They are breaking down barriers of fear and antagonism, and have found a new way to be Church.

As Christians we will want to proclaim the name of Jesus Christ with all our heart, but we must be careful that our evangelism is not dismissed or ignored because our lives and actions do not speak with the same loving commitment which we proclaim. Urban people are well versed in seeing through any pretence. The tenants of the vast housing estate which is Canvey Island are a tough breed who are not easily hoodwinked. The local Church some years ago built a welcoming reception area at the front of their church, trained themselves, staffed the building through the week, and opened it up to all in need. They are all local people themselves, and the quality of the practical care and service they offer is second to none. The project has now been under way for years, and many of those who run it originally came through the door seeking help themselves. It's difficult to be certain why the congregation has grown through the years, but I do know that the Sunday worship is shot through with a sense of what happens in that church from Monday to Saturday. I do not believe that evangelistic preaching is irrelevant, far from it, but I am struck by the growth of those congregations in which there is a clear sense of belonging together to a community which is addressing issues which are of fundamental importance to the lives of people in the locality.

In the Newcastle East Deanery they have set up an Urban Ministry and Theology Project where they seek an integration of three major strands of mission. First, in this very deprived and neglected corner of Newcastle, Jeremy Clark-King is working with the congregations and the local community to co-ordinate the Church's involvement in the regeneration issues that are impacting the parishes. Next, John Sadler is concentrating his efforts on evangelism and the development of the congregations so that they can discover new ways of being the Church in their communities. Finally, Peter Robinson has the task of encouraging theological learning for the whole project and sharing that with others from outside the area – including those training for urban priesthood. All three aspects of the project interconnect and inform one another all the time, and great things develop out of that mutual learning. For all the problems, worries and challenges of urban ministry, our prayers are so often answered, and we witness repeatedly to the God who is the fount of 'the Kingdom, the Power and the Glory'.

*   *   *

Praying the Lord's Prayer, day by day, moment by moment, keeps our hearts and minds centred upon God and upon God's Kingdom. The prayer empowers our imaginations and keeps us true to the story of Jesus so that we, his disciples, can continue his mission in the power of the Spirit and to God's glory. With this Kingdom vision always before us, our small urban congregations, our projects and programmes become, through God's grace, more significant of God's will, and allow us with greater integrity to speak the name of Jesus Christ to an urban world in need.

Part 4

People in Mission

Responding with a Kingdom-based ministry and mission

8 | Street-level Ministry

In accordance with what I understand to be the contextual nature of theology, I began this investigation of urban theology and mission by sharing something of my own context and by telling the urban story from the perspective of the Bible and as it has been told by exponents of the discipline we call urban studies. The second part of this book moved to an analysis of the present urban scene and claimed that, although much has remained the same, within the last fifteen or so years new national and international processes have been affecting it very significantly. In the third part we moved to theological reflection, and became aware of the way in which Jesus' unique ministry grew out of a context which resonates strongly with our present predicament. This prompted us to reflection upon some major themes of his prayer of the Kingdom, the Lord's Prayer. The fourfold process of contextual theology now allows us to move, in this fourth and final part of our study, to look more specifically at how all that has gone before may now be drawn together and issue in a responsive programme and style for urban ministry and mission.

* * *

Walking round an urban parish as a guest of the priest and lay people always gives me a sense of excitement and pride as a Christian. As they walk me along, they point to this street and that, a row of shops there, and on this corner the British Legion next door to the doctor's surgery and the pet shop. Youngsters are larking about by the take-away, and as we walk past, one of them asks the vicar if he's going to bring his guitar to the assembly again next week. 'You've heard the only song I know!' he replies – 'Well, come and sing that one again!' The lay members of our group have lived in the parish for years and know the youngsters' parents. 'That one in the blue's not had it very easy. Has to help his mum, 'cos she's stuck in a wheelchair. He messes about, but he's a good kid really.' We cross the road and stand outside one of the boarded-up shops – 'This is it! What do you think?' They have negotiated with the borough council to open a drop-in centre where they intend to offer computer training during the day, with a social worker attending once a week. They have a parenting course ready that they have piloted in a classroom at the school, but they tell me they can't use the classroom any longer because the head teacher has fallen out with the secretary. It's a long story. In the evenings the residents' association and the Legion will work with the church to staff the centre so that local groups can use it for their meetings. 'The Legion said we should put on some worship each week – their suggestion, mind you!' says Stan with some degree of surprise. 'Come on, my old man runs the social committee – they're not all heathens, you know! We've prayed about this a lot, but what we want to do is make it really matter – not just a shop, but, well . . . you know, a sort of a way of showing that God cares about us here, even if no one else does.'

I am constantly meeting urban Christians who are excited about their lives on the housing estate or in the city. Their ideas are bubbling away and they have a sense of purpose and drive, even if the challenges are huge. On the other hand, there are some urban congregations who know that they are just hanging on as best they can until they are too old to meet each Sunday. They are committed and faithful, but are unsure about what to do. But in most cases, whether full of energy or at the end of their tether, there is always lurking the question, 'Is what we are doing here actually making a difference?' Some clergy have tried everything they know over the years, and to such little effect as they see it, that they are simply waiting for retirement so that they won't have to exhaust themselves any longer. It's true that sometimes the challenges can be overwhelming.

From all that we've described of today's urban scene, we must now try to pull together something of what we have learnt from those who have gone before us, from those who are teaching us today, and from the good work going on in countless urban churches around the country, and indeed the world. Clearly, it will only be possible for me to make a highly subjective choice from all that is percolating up from the pavements of the parishes – but I will enjoy sharing the ideas that I have become excited about, and hope that they will be of service to the reader. I ask forgiveness if I appear to be teaching my grandmother to suck eggs, for some of what I have to say may seem self-evident to those who have long experience of urban ministry. I will sketch an overview of the various issues that I think are of particular importance, and then I will open that up to a more detailed study.

First, it's important to remember where we're coming from and whose we are – we cannot be a useful urban Christian, let alone minister, if we forget to pray, to worship and to sink ourselves in the story of Jesus. But second, like Jesus, we cannot operate alone. In all we do, we need friends – other disciples to be alongside, working as priests and prophets together in critical solidarity with the community in which we are set. All this will be the subject of this chapter – detailing something of the *style* our urban ministry might take.

The actual *processes* of mission, which will form the subject of the next chapter, have to do with listening together to the pulse of the community, hearing the stories and checking them against a more careful analysis of the issues they raise. Discerning what the issues are that are impacting the community can focus the community and bring together people of goodwill. But we will also have something very distinctive to offer as Christians, and we will want to bring that faith component into the mix. This is the dynamic from which can emerge a deeper sense of community and all manner of community programmes which will hopefully not merely deal with symptoms but address the underlying issues. This can be a real occasion for thanksgiving, as befits the 'eucharistic community'. But even the best programme of Christian action can miss the mark if under-taken with the wrong attitude, so we begin by asking what style is most appropriate for urban ministry today.

Knowing whose we are

It will always be important for urban Christians to retain a sense of who they are and to whom they belong, and that is only done by placing our-selves in God's presence. In this way, what we do and how we live our urban lives can be open, amid all the clamour and noise that surrounds us, to the Word of God in the midst of it all. We put ourselves daily before our God, in whatever manner works for us, intentionally opening ourselves up to an awareness of that Holiness which is the gift of Godself to us. We draw together to read and meditate upon the story of Jesus, and let prayer heighten our awareness of God's incarnation in our midst.

Biding God's time

Urban prayer is not a new thing. We are told in Genesis 18 that Abraham prayed for the city of Sodom and negotiated a deal with God – that even if only a small group of people in the city could be shown to live upright lives, then their presence would save the whole city. Even in those early searching days of faith, our forebears seem to have cottoned on to the fact that it only takes a small ember of love and justice to be kept burning in the city for it to receive God's blessing and approval. Just a small flame of love and witness will do it.

But this story of Abraham's determined prayer also teaches us to put some bite into our urban praying. Stuart Kimber and his family live in the vicarage in a very run-down part of Southend. He and his wife and their friends have gathered together many facts about the conurbation – unemployment and mortality figures, addiction and crime, youth centres and hospices, sorrows and joys – and have presented all this information in very manageable booklet form, and sent it round to all the churches in the area so that when people pray for Southend, they can do so from a realistic and informed basis. Urban prayer, like Abraham's, must be informed, compassionate and full of hope.

Informed urban prayer should not be the sort of self-absorbed spirituality which is found in 'Mind and Spirit' bookshops, but prayer which alerts us to the deeper concerns of God for the issues we face. Through it God enables us with the stability and courage we will need to address those issues, and opens up our imagination so that the Holy Spirit can blow away the cobwebs of the old cultures which might be constraining our Kingdom thinking.

When we pray for people and things in our urban environment, we begin to see them no longer from our own perspective, but from God's perspective – with all their potential for good, and with possibilities for change and an open future. This in turn helps us to become more hopeful and more compassionate beings, less liable to demonize others, but also more determined to see things change for the better. Sometimes placing ourselves in the presence of the Holy One can save us from ourselves. We may suddenly realize that it's not 'me' who should be running this project, or perhaps we sense that we are not honouring our neighbours as we should – not listening sufficiently or allowing them their dignity and self-respect. Sometimes it will feel worse than that, and our Bible study or prayer will leave us feeling we have no answers, no way through, that we are just human beings and not God – a negative and tough way into truth, but a way which often results from deep prayer.

We cannot always be with others at prayer time or in Bible study, so on some days it may be a more solitary business. But people in the community should still know that it's happening – we can ring the church bell if we have one – so they can join in where they are, and so that they know we're not in any way reluctant to engage with them about matters 'spiritual'.

They will quite rightly want to know that we are seeking to place ourselves before God every day, and praying for them too.

We rejoice to see so many urban churches which have a full programme of worship, their halls full of meetings of lunch-clubs, pensioners' and young people's groups and projects, all designed to serve the needy and to help build community. This is highly to be commended, but there is an additional option which would make that fine ministry even more significant, and which is available even to those congregations where it is simply not possible to have such a marvellous array of activity. This more ambitious way of operating is a way of being Church together which, as its first concern, looks at all we do from the perspective of *metanoia*-repentance. This call to radical Kingdom of God awareness asks of us that together we look beyond the outward appearance to see the underlying causes and cultures which have to be addressed in ourselves and in society, so that God's will may be done and the Lord's Prayer fulfilled. It is in fact to model our discipleship as much as possible upon the dynamic ministry of our Lord Jesus. Founded upon that experience of God in the midst, it works by seeking to understand the powers and cultures of our urban context and setting up acted parables and sacramental signs of the alternative Kingdom – witnessing to that deeper righteousness and grace which underpins the cultural values of the Kingdom of God.

The New Testament Church was called to do this in the cities of the Roman Empire, and for generations thereafter its vocation was to the city. Just like the Greeks and Romans before them, the early missionary Christians intentionally went from urban settlement to urban settlement, creating enclaves within them of groups committed to the Kingdom. Through its long history, God has called his Church to 'stay in the city', and to use that presence as the springboard for mission. When the Jesuits moved into South America and Asia, they used the same urban strategy, and where there was not already a town or city to mission from, they founded one. The vast cities of São Paulo in Brazil, and Nagasaki in Japan, were both founded by the Jesuits as mission stations. The question that each of us should therefore ask ourselves must be, 'Is God calling me to urban mission?' It will not be everybody's calling of course, but neither should it be evaded by those who do have the gifts to offer. Mine was an urban vocation for nearly fifty years of my life, and not one moment do I regret. The wonder of living alongside and learning from the people of the estate and the inner city, both rich and poor, meeting God in situations of poverty and deprivation, in celebrations of life and in the deep issues of our society, has given me and my family such a rich experience which, for us, I think would not have been possible anywhere else.

The last nine years have been a call for me to live outside the city and from there I have learnt how both the suburban and the rural life of Britain are also intimately related to the powerful influences and pressures of the city. I now have no doubt that we live in a culture which has been overwhelmed by the urban, and therefore God needs those whom he calls to hear that call and offer themselves for the excitement and challenge of living the Kingdom in the urban regions of Britain.

There to serve

Kingdom of God theology is not just a great crossword puzzle in the sky. My father would say of academic theology, 'It may be true, son, but if it doesn't work, then why bother?' It seems fair to judge that to have integrity, an idea must have power to deliver on its promises. But power can be dominating, even demonic, and the power of God's Kingdom is anything but. I will always remember, in one small urban Bible study, we were reading the Bible's description of Jesus on trial before the Sanhedrin, the Jewish religious court. As if to deny the authority which their law court had over him, Jesus is reluctant to answer their questions. 'Mind you,' said Edna, 'what we've got here is not a passive Jesus at all. He really speaks out, but in a powerfully loving way. It's more of a bold humility, isn't it? To stand up there in that awe-inspiring religious court-room and lay it on the line – that's very powerful indeed; but it's not self-acclamation. It's bold humility.' That must mean, Colin responded, that 'our servanthood is very acceptable to his power.' Power in our urban world is an ever-present issue, and is difficult to handle.

People who like to help can be quite overpowering. It is as if their need to help derives from a deep-seated urge to have people dependent upon them. Of course, to give is usually much more enjoyable than to receive, but if every time we meet a friend we have to have a present for them, then the relationship is unhealthy. So, although it is often the way that helping agencies are expected to operate, we must take care that in our ministry we never concentrate above all else upon people's needs and our own power to help them. To begin with, it is crippling for them to have their needs the only object of other people's attention, as if their weakness were their identity. Second, when we persist in reinforcing a person's need by our constant reference to it, they never have a chance to escape from it. When Jesus releases the paralytic from his illness, he tells him to take up his bed and carry it away – no longer dependent on his friends, nor even upon Jesus, to carry him. Jesus empowers.

The office of deacon in the Church is a most significant role, for the deacon teaches the Church about servanthood and models that for a world which has in the past been prone to abuse people through its helping agencies. The discovery of the gifts and strengths of those who are usually seen as 'the needy' can be a thrilling experience. My last parish was very 'needy', but within the congregation were pavement poets and artists of real ability, there were singers and actors, secretaries, skilled labourers, teachers and mothers, taxi-drivers, musicians, cooks, nurses, story-tellers, and so it went on. Some knew all about physical and mental illness from bitter personal experience, they knew lots about addiction, domestic violence, unemployment, and also how to celebrate with exuberance the good things of life. Some had skills to hand on to others in a formal way, others were happy to share more informally, and all held an intimate knowledge of what made the neighbourhood tick, how to persevere under the urban stresses and strains, and survive come what may.

There was an amazing array of skills, but it would have been very easy to make people keep their skills to themselves, or even convince them that they had no skills at all.[1] There are still the vestiges of a 'father knows best' mentality among some clergy, and that goes for all 'churchmanships' and both genders! That attitude may incline worshippers to treat their clergy with rather more deference than they deserve, but the outcome is that, while the cleric may think everyone is in full agreement, when the testing moment comes, congregational support falls away. It is all too easy to use one's power to de-skill and not to empower.

In February 2002, I received a letter from a dear friend, Jenny Richardson, then Training Co-ordinator of Unlock, the urban training project. She was writing to me about the MA research she had undertaken. 'I was trying to find out what sort of skills and background people needed, if they were going to be a radical theological educator. What was clear by the end was that the most important thing that people bring to the job is their attitude – especially valuing people. Sounds obvious, but at least I can now quote the research when I'm talking with people about how this is more important than, for example, being a brilliant Bible scholar.' I believe Jenny to be absolutely right, that if urban people know that they are valued and are not simply being used by the minister, then all sorts of gifts will burgeon and thrive – gifts of the Spirit.

A tough urban environment can be disabling enough, without that being added to by an overpowering minister who only pretends to serve. If an urban discipleship group is going to be involved in any way with regeneration projects, for example, it will find itself immersed in complex government jargon, continually changing criteria, cryptic acronyms, a plethora of programmes and a multitude of government and other professionals. It is enough to scare the living daylights out of anyone. In the face of all these challenges we as ministers are inclined to seek the safety of something we feel more in control of. But we are not called to duck the issues, wherever we may be located. St John the Divine was on Patmos, a Roman concentration camp, when, at the beginning of his Revelation, he referred to himself as 'your brother and partner in hardships, in the kingdom and in perseverance in Jesus'. We are in good Christian company when we find things hard going, for like the saints who went before us, we live in the overlap between the 'now' and the 'not yet' of the Kingdom of God. This will cost us – but whenever did love not cost? Bishop Jim Thompson proved very helpful to me on many occasions when I was a parish priest in east London. He told me, when I was frustrated that a parish project was moving so slowly, 'Laurie, you must learn "strategic patience" in your ministry'. We are called to stand at the foot of the cross and observe the Christ undertaking his powerful work, not barge in and make it all happen our way. Knowing whose we are in urban ministry will keep leading us back to prayer and meditation upon the central issue of power.

We do not work alone

After many years sunk in the experience of his people, Jesus moves into overt ministry and mission and immediately surrounds himself with a group with whom he shares his vision. They were men and women who brought with them a cross-section of worldly experience, as well as all the muddle and tension that beset human relationships. Judging by that group, we do not need to be too worried if our congregations are small and not filled with professional people, but they do need to have a discipleship commitment to learning more about the Kingdom. Many urban churches do not attract large numbers and so we do well to learn from rural churches how small congregations can have their own dynamics.[2] They often tend towards a rather tribal style so that, rather than addressing and analysing difficulties, they are simply lived with until they issue somehow in a sense of resolution. Small churches tend to be defensive and conservative because they are concerned about their survival and anything that rocks the boat could send them under. The key is to listen carefully, win trust and go for long-term advances, rather than fight short-term battles. Each one of us, but particularly the incoming minister, will be likely to be misunderstood from time to time – saying the wrong thing, or upsetting a delicate balance – and this can lead to problems for all, so it is always recommended that we have a skilled and experienced urban mentor with whom we can talk things through. The Church of England has the mutual support system of the deanery chapter to assist and, if used well, the experience and wisdom of the other clergy can be very supportive.

We do have to make sure that our urban congregation or group does not become isolated or inward-looking. We will often find that there are other voluntary associations and clubs around who will be grateful for a connection with the congregation, and who share a concern for the neighbourhood. Issue groups too will have access to helpful information and may have links with national and international networks. Homelessness projects, the racial equality council, ecology clubs, political, educational and hobby groups, may all be hidden away in the community. As our work progresses we will want to network with groups such as these, and early contact can help pave the way for that later, more intensive collaboration. Every Saturday, outside the Tarpots pub, the local congregation sets up a booth on the pavement for passers-by and shoppers who can look in and be provided with contact names of all sorts of local groups and organizations. Problems are shared too and the local MP drops by when he can. It's such a simple project, but has become the envy of lots of the market traders – and all those Christians are doing is sharing their network with anyone who wants to know. They are also making sure that their congregation does not become isolated within its own churchy concerns.

Sharing with others always teaches us so much. It was instructive to hear from Canon Fred Williams, when I visited him in New York, that when the local congregational leaders in Harlem decided to get together to fight for an improvement in their community, they initially met with failure. Eventually their congregational members sat them down and challenged them. They pointed out that what was impeding their progress was that each leader wanted to be king of the community. They had to put the needs of their own personal charisma aside. Fred explained how, from then on, the leaders covenanted with one another only to work for the furtherance of the community as a whole, and to rein in their competitive spirit. With one another's prayer and support, Harlem Congregations for Community Improvement Inc. has gone from strength to strength.

Strong ecumenical relationships between urban congregations can be a source of great support and a seed-bed for new creativity and ideas. For eleven years of my life I had the privilege of serving a combined urban congregation of Methodists and Anglicans, with a few Catholics and URC Christians for good measure, and it proved to be one of the most productive periods of my ministry. In Britain, we sometimes find that, apart from the Anglicans and Roman Catholics, the mainstream denominations have become so weak they have pulled out of the poor urban areas altogether. But where mainstream denominations are weakening, the incoming communities often bring their own dynamic religion with them and set up pentecostal congregations which have significant impact on the area. On one occasion I was pleased to receive an invitation to the opening ceremonies of a new Black Pentecostal Church and, having been asked to preach, took along as a sign of our unity the gift of a Bible. I could not understand why they were reluctant to accept my gift, since I had spent a lot of money on a large leather-bound Bible in modern English. Of course, in my naivety, what I had not then realized was that many incoming churches have an extremely conservative theology and sense of purity, and I had upset the purity of their new building by bringing into it something other than the King James Version of the Bible. We certainly live and learn when we seek to work together – but in the end the benefits are tremendous.

The community as priest

In the Hebrew scriptures, the priest is the one who enters the Holy of Holies and touches the sacred things on behalf of the people of God. In urban ministry and mission, the whole Christian community enters into urban experiences and finds there the presence of the Holy One – touching upon people's lives and cultures with all care and solemnity. The ordained priest today knows that you cannot be a priest by yourself – it is always a collective enterprise, undertaken with the eucharistic community as it handles sacred things together. Working-class cultures can help in this regard by teaching us to handle leadership corporately, for leadership there is often held by groups rather than by individuals. To get one person to be the treasurer, for example, may prove to be an insuperable problem, whereas a small group may be quite prepared to take it on. So also, priesthood is a community undertaking, while the individual, if there is an ordained person in the midst, focuses that for all. The ordained priest is there to make sure the group remains focused aright, but the whole group enters the Holy of Holies and does the 'celebrating'. And just as the ordained priest has the role of presiding at the transformation of the bread into the Body of Christ, so too the priest must watch for the transformation of those who receive that bread that they themselves may become more readily the Body of Christ. The ordained person has the tricky job of watching out for every possibility of transformation in the community, wherever there may be the signs of the Kingdom coming to be. It is the deacon's job to prepare the holy table at the Communion feast – in other words, to spend time in preparing for, and so encouraging the signs of transformation to occur. So all the ordained within the local Christian group must make sure that things are in readiness and that the group's focus is on seeing holy things come to light in the midst of the ordinary 'bread and wine' of urban life. At the Holy Communion we share our bread, and watch for Christ to usher in the Kingdom, as we share Christ's priesthood in the midst of a needy world. As Jesus said to his disciples, 'I shall not eat it until it is fulfilled in the Kingdom of God.'

As the Christian community enacts the Kingdom Supper in remembrance of Jesus, through the priest they perform four key actions, in taking bread, blessing it, breaking it and finally sharing it together. It is helpful therefore to look at the significance of these four key actions as they instruct us in our urban ministry and mission.

1. Taking the bread

As we bring our daily bread to be offered at the Communion, so we are symbolically bringing our very selves and all that we are in community. We bring our stories – the fragments of all our experience of God in our midst. The bread is a symbolic offering of our gifts, of ourselves and of the cultures that make us who we are. We bring our listening – our hearing of the stories and perceptions of all those around the community. We will have sought to learn the language of the community, be it the language of the poor, of the rich, of the planners and developers, or whoever it may be. All the stories of the people are welcome at the table of Jesus, and as people come, they are invited to bring their very selves to the table, and are promised a listening welcome. The eucharistic community brings all this to its Kingdom feast.

2. Blessing the bread

Having carefully gathered together the story of the community and its people, the next action of the Communion is that the community gives thanks to God for all that has been brought. The bread is held out and honoured as a gift from God, and to God. We hold the stories and the lives of our community before the living God, and as we seek to respect and honour them, we ask God to take them and bless them – making them more pure and wholesome. We have gathered the stories because we truly believe that each, even the lowliest, is worthy of our attention if ever we are to learn what God is truly about in our community. To do that we will have to critique one another's contribution, but we do not do that until they have been honoured and blessed as a true and acceptable offering to God.

3. Breaking the bread

Once the bread is offered, blessed and received as worthy, then it can be broken open – sacrificed to the rigours of Christian scrutiny. Each story is broken now in order that we can rid it of its demons, of its stereotyping, of its unjust biases or error, so that it may become a more worthy offering. As the bread is broken open, so we begin to analyse the issues which emerge from all that has been brought to the table. We check the data, comparing each contribution and perspective with the next and with our Christian traditions of faith. The developer's story of a vision for a complete rebuilding of the estate may jar with stories of those whose community it is – and who just love living there but want better facilities and decent incomes rather than the developer's grandiose schemes. As the bread is broken in the Eucharist, so our issues are scrutinized in the light of the gospel and we see the judgement of the Lord, present in our midst.

4. Sharing the bread

We have brought our bread, our very selves, to the table, we have blessed and reverenced each story and the person who has brought it, and we have broken open our experience in the light of the Christian story. Now the bread is shared.

When I was a young boy I hitch-hiked to Greece and one Sunday attended a church service in a small Greek village. At the very end of the Eucharist we were each given a piece of bread from a large basket by the door, and we took it with us out into the community to share with everyone we met – people passing by in the street, in the café, by the bus-stop. The experience of the Eucharist was being shared out far and wide into the community at large. For the Eucharist is not a confined action, held captive by the Church, but is the place of regeneration for the whole community – the whole created order. Geoff and Kate King had a God-given dream for a youth project that would help local youngsters on the Flower Estate in Sheffield experience how they could be really productive in their community. Geoff and Kate were so taken with their dream that they shared it with all and sundry, and their 'Dream Scheme' proved a great boon to the youngsters of their community for more than eight years. The blessings of the eucharistic community are there to be shared with all the neighbourhood.

The four actions of the Eucharist remind us that as we engage in urban ministry so we are priests together, celebrating the grace of God in our midst. We are handling sacred things and together are made into the very Body of Christ. And as that Body of Christ, we partake moment by moment in the changes to our community which will signal that God's will is being done here, on earth as it is in heaven. Time and again we will see the marks of the Kingdom being built around those four actions of the Eucharist – just as they have determined the four sections of this book.

The community as prophet

It is only after the Christian discipleship group has become priestly that it can become truly prophetic – we have to take and receive and listen before we can give voice to what we have heard. There is a wonderful Bible story in Numbers 22, of a prophet who is tempted to speak before he has listened. The King of Moab promised to shower gifts upon him if he, Balaam, will curse the Hebrew nation. So Balaam saddles up his ass and goes off as if to curse. But even the ass is aware that this is not the thing to do and has to make that plain to the prophet! Even an ass knows that you don't speak prophetic words until you've listened carefully to God to know what must be said. Attentive priestly listening comes before the discipleship group can proclaim the Word of the Lord. In the brief survey of urban ministry and mission which we offered in Chapter 3, we mentioned a number of charismatic prophetic figures, but they only deserve mention because they immersed themselves first in their communities for many attentive years before they spoke out so vigorously.

Prophets can be frightened

Elijah, the Hebrew prophet, has much to teach us. The cycle of events is recorded for us in the first book of Kings, where we see him challenging the Ba'al worship that surrounded the court of King Ahab and his wife Jezebel. Elijah defeats the prophets of Ba'al, but for his pains he receives a threat from Jezebel, and we are told 'he was afraid and fled for his life'.

Violence and the fear of violence keeps many people from responding to an urban vocation. The streets can be filthy, the public services negligible, insurance costs prohibitive, and local schools poor. It is no good being naively romantic about these challenges, for the dangers and the deprivation do exist. And yet that is not the only reality. My experience of visiting and living in dangerous cities around the world has been that as soon as I have my suitcase unpacked so that I have some investment in the place as my home, and once I get to know local faces and become known around, then things begin to feel altogether different. The fear begins to subside once we know the local shopkeepers, and we soon learn from the locals who can be trusted and what streets are best only visited during the day. One learns to act sensibly as one becomes street-wise to that particular locality.

I think the most dangerous city I have ever visited is Rio de Janeiro. Life is very cheap there and a visit to the bus station at night is the experience of a lifetime. I journeyed on the last bus through the city with Michael, intending to catch the night coach from the bus station back to his home in São Paulo. Suddenly the bus began to fly along at a fearfully dangerous speed and the crowded passengers clung on for their lives as we negotiated the tight corners of the back-street route to the bus station. Michael leaned over with a glorious smile on his face and said, 'The driver has to go this fast because otherwise the bus will be attacked by bandits and we'll all get robbed – or something worse.' The news was alarming, but what stuck in my mind was his gleaming smile. Indeed, everyone on the bus seemed equally to be enjoying the craziness of the speeding journey, shouting out to the driver and joking together about how they were being jostled as the antiquated bus threw them all into one another's laps. The danger of bandits was palpable, but urban fear also creates an odd togetherness which is hard to explain.

The cities of Israel/Palestine are violent too, and one watches with incredulous admiration the children happily playing amid the rubble of their bulldozed streets. Of all the places in the world to choose to have your first baby, it would never be Bethlehem – but Jesus is born there and accepts that challenging vocation. Our own cities and housing estates do not seem, at first sight, to be the right places to bring up our children if we have the option of ministering instead in an affluent suburb, within reach of a 'good' school. And yet, even if we are only interested in academic attainment, some of our very best schools are undoubtedly urban institutions. But people of faith are hopefully aware that education means a lot more than 'getting the grades'. Urban children often become very street-wise and understand the plight of others with a knowing awareness which other children never attain. They learn to appreciate and use the cosmopolitan opportunities of their surroundings as they grow older, and find that they have accrued a rich and exciting education, that might otherwise not have been the case.

On the other hand, some children are not robust enough to cope with urban street life and schooling, and it has to be admitted that being the child of a minister is not an easy burden to bear in some quarters. Clergy are alongside other professionals such as nurses and the police in wearing a discernible, visible uniform, and this does indeed make clergy targets for attack and abuse. This exposure does however put us alongside those millions of God's children who experience this vulnerability as a matter of routine – and it puts us alongside Christ himself, who is even accepting of crucifixion in order to show his love for the poor. However, most of us would also testify that there are many benefits in urban mission for both clergy and their families which far outweigh any of the small sacrifices, and are a handsome compensation for them.

Prophets get low

Elijah had fled because of his fear of violence, but once he had escaped, another emotion began to overwhelm him. '"Yahweh," he says, "I have had enough. Take my life; I am no better than my ancestors." Then he lay down and went to sleep' (1 Kings 19.4). When we first take up our ministry, we may feel that we are going to change the world in a way that our forebears simply never managed. We therefore arrive in our parish, or amid the project, full of excitement and energy. There is an initial rush of fascination with the culture, the sights and the challenges that surround us. But after that initial rush and perhaps early success, some then experience more negative and depressive feelings. Sometimes it may be that we are frustrated that progress is so slow, or our schemes and bids for funding are falling through. Maybe at first the spontaneity of the place enthralled us, but now we see that same casual immediacy as a disorganized lack of determination which won't get things done. We could even make the crass assumption that our own culture was in some way superior, just because we miss it so. This assumption is so dangerous because it can disable our ministry very significantly. If we are not urban by birth and breeding, we may simply miss the ways we've been used to. When I moved ten years ago to the outer suburbs of London, for the first time in my life I saw the coming and going of the seasons. In the city it just got dustier in summer and more slippery in winter, but this was a revelation! My wife Vicki, a country girl by birth, said, 'Oh, how I've missed this all these years.' And I never knew.

We may even feel stressed out and exhausted by the relentless pressure and grind of a tough urban ministry. It is then that we can feel, like Elijah, simply not up to the task. As a priest in the East End, my parish included many of the old parishes in which had ministered some of the heroic inner-city slum priests of past generations. I was lent a book which had been written by a woman in her old age, in which she described her experiences of being brought up as the child of one of those local heroes. Her stories were fascinating and a wonderful witness to her remarkable father. But amid the pages it became clear that her father had also been prone to periods of exhaustion and despair and often had to escape to the country-side to regain his composure and vitality. What a welcome and reassuring book that was! To know that even the heroes of old had their times, like Elijah, when it was all too much.

Some of those Anglo-Catholic slum priests had the advantage of having religious communities of nuns or friars around them for support and encouragement – and we of course are running on an empty tank if we believe that we can be in ministry on our own. We have emphasized already how important it is to follow Christ's example and work together with others in discipleship groups. I suspect that the episode at Caesarea Philippi, which is so richly recorded for us in the Gospels (Mark 8.27–30), tells of a moment in Christ's ministry when he really felt in need of their support and reassuring counsel: 'Who do people say that I am?' I believe that the ordained minister does well to ask that same question of the discipleship group to which she or he belongs. To gather with a small group who know us well and ask them to appraise our ministry can be a wonderfully creative, if daunting experience. The way I used to do it was to ask them to list what they believed my role and functions as the vicar should be, while I did the same thing in another room. We would then come together and swap notes. What a revelation that was! Expectations were usually quite unrealistic on both sides and a good conversation ironed out many of the inhuman assumptions. After agreeing a more manageable list, we then parted again and they gave me scores out of ten for each item. Acknowledging the limitations of the schema, it was still salutary to learn that people really did appreciate one's attempts where it mattered, and were only too keen to be helpful and supportive, albeit honest, about the shortcomings. My work seemed so much more focused after that experience, and amazingly, lots of the stress just evaporated.

It is so important for clergy in particular to remember that we are no different from others. We too need space and time away from the job, as much as we love it and gain so much from it. It is when we find ourselves trying to please people all the time, or on the contrary, not being able to be compassionate and sensitive, that we should know we are not functioning well. There is then a tendency to believe that we need more skills in order to deal with the situation and the stress, but my experience tells me that it's not so much more skills that we need, but more prayer and more parties. Space to be quietly with God, and space to be noisy with friends, brings us back to a proper sense of where our priorities should be, and an appreciation of our own need for re-creation. I find that God, friends and a good mentor can usually do the trick.

For some, however, the strains of urban ministry really do become too much and health begins to tell. It is important to monitor ourselves and our colleagues, so that we do not leave it too late, but have a break when we need it. Christ himself sought out quiet places, and those clergy who believe themselves to be superior to the need to get away should think again. If things get very bad, there are often structures to support and assist, and there is nothing 'unholy' about acknowledging our need for support. Some ministers who have been born and bred in the area can still be prone to burn-out, and should not be assumed by others, or assume themselves, to be above the need to seek refuge when the need arises. We simply must learn to be honest with ourselves and acknowledge our need of God and one another if we are to be useful and faithful urban ministers. It was only when Elijah hit rock bottom and acknowledged his need, that God was able to open him up to the most profound experience of his life – an encounter with the Holy One in the 'still small voice', amidst the earthquake and hurricane. The same can happen for us.

Prophets are imaginative

Although I have concentrated on the problems that ordained ministers may encounter, I do not believe that it is only the ordained who have to deal with these issues, nor, heaven forbid, that the prophetic task only falls to the ordained. On the contrary, the lone prophet who fails to be surrounded by a community of faith can often be a deluded voice – lacking both integrity and clarity of insight. The Hebrew prophets very often had their prophetic bands around them, but also, they were often able to think 'outside the box' because they were not constrained too much by the fetters of the institution they sought to serve. Modern urban prophets can often find themselves in a similar situation.

When it is clear that the church building is no longer working for the community, or when the style of liturgy is no longer a helpful vehicle for the people's worship, it has then become clear that one simply must begin thinking 'outside the box'. The prophetic group must be open therefore to the constant prompting of the Holy Spirit – who so often acts unconstitutionally. St Paul's Church in Bordesley Green, Birmingham, was built in the 1960s but had become a cold barn of a place. The congregation was not, however, down-hearted by the challenge, but being aware of the tremendous needs of the area decided to stop worrying about the church building and open a community café instead. The Crossover Café became the focus for an employment resource centre, child care facilities and a youth project. The success of the café allowed them to look back to the church building and to think much more creatively. They changed its interior so that many different group activities and meetings could take place there. When our buildings are so very bad, we simply have to do more exciting and imaginative things with them. There's nothing to lose, so we can talk with developers about a complete rethink of the plant. We can even imagine what it would be like to work from a completely different base altogether. In Southend, the Bar 'n' Bus youth project has decided, with the support of local churches, to reach out to young people at risk from drugs and homelessness. They use an old double-decker bus to meet in, rather than the local church buildings. The real challenge however is what happens next, because those youngsters who come to a Christian faith on the Bus will never go near any of the local churches – even those with lively worship – because the culture there is so inappropriate for them.

Prophets ask critical questions

Prophetic urban groups ask the critical questions of the Church at large, just as the prophets of old challenged the religion of Israel – are we a truly sharing Church, prepared to risk; or a defensive outfit, stuck in the past, hiding our skills and fearful of being hurt or changed? But the prophet must also challenge the wider community and the nation at large where necessary. Archaeology tells us that Hebrew prophecy really came to maturity when the disparity between the rich and poor became evident in the cities. When we realize that today the poorest forty-eight countries of the world have a combined income equal to the combined incomes of the three richest individuals of the world, then we know just how crass the injustice and how intense the need for prophecy in our own generation.

Martin Luther King Jr said that although the Church is expected to be the servant of the state, in fact it has a duty to be its conscience. But there can be no 'us and them' here, for the judgement which the Church's prophecy lays upon the nation must also be heard as a judgement upon itself. We must seek to adopt a 'critical solidarity' in our prophetic work, not holding ourselves up as some pure guiding light, but as equally under the scrutiny of the word we proclaim. This will certainly require courage and fortitude as we embolden ourselves to speak the truth to community leaders, local authorities, business and voluntary organizations, and to the Church.

On the other hand, urban prophecy is not without its rewards. In Isaiah 58 we read,

> Shout for all you are worth, do not hold back, raise your voice like a trumpet . . . Is this not the sort of fast that pleases me: to break unjust fetters, to let the oppressed go free, . . . sharing your food with the hungry, sheltering the homeless poor . . . ? Then your light will blaze out like the dawn and your wound be quickly healed over . . . You will be called 'Breach-mender', 'Restorer of streets to be lived in'.

Here Isaiah forecasts that if we engage in the prophetic task, working to see justice prevail, then our own wounds will be healed – we ourselves will receive the gift of wholeness, and what's more, in honouring others we in turn will receive a fine urban accolade: 'Restorer of streets to be lived in.' What honour could be finer? Our stance of critical solidarity puts us under the same judgement as others, but it also brings us the same mutual healing when the Word is heard.

The street juggler

For the urban Christian community to think of itself in mission as priest and prophet can, I believe, be quite helpful. But there are many other paradigms which equally might serve. Some like to think of the minister as the conductor of an orchestra, not playing an instrument but knowing how to bring the musical talents of the players to bear upon the score, so that harmony and direction inspire the resultant performance. This picture emphasizes the group nature of the enterprise but does not, I fear, quite ring true for most urban ministry. The conductor seems a little too removed from the action, and an orchestra usually has more instrumentalists than we can muster. I worked for a short while loading lorries in a warehouse. I was surprised to find how harmoniously the men worked and what high regard they had for Mr Robertson, their supervisor. One Tuesday morning I came in early to find Mr Robertson cleaning the men's toilets – apparently he did it every week. I've never forgotten that fine example of leadership. Likewise in urban ministry leadership, there's a lot of 'mucking in' involved.

The urban minister will undoubtedly be inundated by a whole host of tasks, each one enough to overwhelm many a mortal. An Anglican may typically have a hundred or so funerals to do each year and perhaps quite a few baptisms and weddings, each requiring visiting and preparation. There may be five or more schools to visit, plus hospitals, prisons, factories, offices and shops – and that's before you start counting the population who once upon a time would each have expected a visit. In addition to all that, urban ministers have to keep up to date on government urban policy, and know how to work with local government, shopkeepers, landlords, action groups, worshipping congregations, prayer groups, volunteers who don't turn up, awkward people who seem to attend everything, the demands of the denominational structures and school governing bodies, the demands of family and friends, their own needs for sustenance and recreation, administration, complicated data, crumbling buildings, and so the list goes on. At times, for all the determination to be collaborative in ministry, it can feel like a lonely ride.

This is why it is so important to create appropriate ways of dealing with all the business by developing a collaborative framework. No one person can be expected to take all this on alone, and it is not fair either to expect one person to make the terrifying decisions about what elements will have to be jettisoned – because it will inevitably be the case that something will have to go. It is most important that this matter is honestly and openly dealt with by the Christian community acting together. In my own experience I have found the appraisal exercise I described a little earlier to be a useful way to share the issues and to settle upon an agreed and manageable way of working. But there is also a whole variety of parish structures to choose from which can help the congregation to share the decision-making and executive load. 'Every member ministry' schemes, sub-committee and working group structures, ministry leadership teams, and so on, are all there to help – but it is important to settle upon the one that best suits the cultural milieu within which the Christian community operates. Charles Handy's little gem, *Understanding Voluntary Organisations*,[3] can help to steer us to the appropriate structural style.

But even when a structure is successfully set up, many professional urban ministers will still feel themselves going under because of all the calls upon them. Somehow our model of urban ministry leadership has to steer between the reality of meagre resources and the nonsense of the minister trying to do it all alone. Once, when I was walking through the streets of

Berlin, my eye was taken by a street entertainer – a clown who stood in front of a huge pile of coloured balls. He began to throw one very large yellow ball into the air until a few of us had gathered around. He communicated with his audience by squeaks and whistles, but we soon understood that he was promising that he would juggle all the balls at once. He took up a second large ball and soon that too was flying high. A third he only just managed to keep aloft, but as he looked at the pile remaining he became very dismayed and great spurts of tears came spraying from his eyes. Then a great idea seemed to strike him and he began convincing members of the crowd to help him by throwing the other balls to one another. Anyone who did not co-operate became soaked by his tears. One way or another he cajoled ten or so of us to take part, until all the balls were aloft. Then he became visibly sorrowful that he did not have enough balls for other members of his audience, so while we continued at his command, he had them fishing in their pockets and shopping bags for likely items that they could toss into the air. Eventually people were even taking off their trainers and throwing them up. And in all the fun, games and hilarity, it slowly dawned on everyone that our juggler had discarded his clown costume and merged invisibly into the crowd. I felt that juggler had a lot to teach me. Despite the fact that he evidently could not juggle all the balls at once, he helped the community to have faith that it could be done, despite all the evidence. And because of that faith, we all saw the evidence transformed before our eyes.

9 | Moving into Urban Mission

Having described something of the style of life and ministry we would hope for in the urban minister, we now move on to describe the process of urban mission itself, seeking once again to conform all we do to Kingdom principles. We must be cautious to note however that because we have divided the style of ministry and the processes of mission into separate chapters for ease of discussion, this should not lead us to suppose that they can be separated in practice. I do not believe we can separate 'being' from 'doing'; they must always act together in our journey of 'becoming' the Christian community which the Kingdom of God requires. In other words, this chapter and the last are best seen as two ways of describing the same thing – the life of Christian work and witness in our urban settings.

In all we do throughout the processes of urban mission we must hold the Kingdom of God as our touchstone for ministry as well as for all our analysis, reflection and action. If we fail to do this, then, with luck, we may become an adequate social care agency or political lobby group, but not necessarily one which reflects the life and teaching of our Lord Jesus Christ – and that means we will simply not be 'Church'. Once again therefore we must begin with prayer and worship.

Worshipping together

Good urban liturgy can be a great source of sustenance, but it can also be the springboard to theological vision. Praising God together in the midst of a difficult and confining situation, raises our sights so that while others cry, 'There is no alternative', the worshipping community will reply, 'But of course there is an alternative, we meet it here every Sunday!' The Lord's Prayer begins in awe, with the words, 'Our Father, which art in heaven, hallowed be thy name', and this attitude of praise and wonder puts everything in proper perspective and reminds us that all else, including the dominant urban myths of turbo-capitalism, are secondary. By seeing Jesus in the breaking of the bread we accustom our eye to seeing God's presence in the most unlikely places – in a small piece of bread, or in the brokenness of our own urban community. David Ford and Al McFadyen[1] call this process 'praising open' the situation, allowing God's light to shine into our imagination so that we see new possibilities. So praise and worship can be not only a wonderful antidote to the drab captivity of a stinking stairwell and a damp flat, but also a glimpse of what is yet to be – the alternative that is possible!

Sitting in St Peter's church one evening, my attention was drawn to a young man who sat on a chair amid a group of other youngsters. As the service progressed I began to realize that he was suffering from Tourette Syndrome, that acute mental illness which prompts one to shout obscenities uncontrollably. From time to time the young man would lose control, swear very loudly, and then slap his own face in self-recrimination. I saw a young woman in the group lean over and put her arm consolingly around him to comfort him in his distress and shame, and to assure him that his presence was welcomed and his problem understood by the other young worshippers. I would have thought that the intrusion of such extreme obscenities in the midst of worship would have marred the whole occasion, and yet on the contrary, it became for us all a very significant mark of God's compassion in the midst of profound suffering. The worship enabled us to 'praise open' the situation and go beyond our own limited vision and shared brokenness.

Many of our eucharistic liturgies are far too wordy and highbrow to be appropriate for congregations in deeply urban areas. In Los Angeles I once attended a jazz Mass where words were kept to an absolute minimum. Eminent jazz musicians created in music the whole eucharistic service, without the use of words at all. The priest enacted the shape of the liturgy at the altar as the music inspired him, and we all received in silence. The experience taught me how limiting and constraining words can sometimes be, even though our liturgists love to multiply them. Among most urban congregations there will be at least a few people who find reading painful, if not impossible. I was myself not able to read properly until I was into my late teens and I remember how humiliating and isolating church attendance could sometimes be for me, simply because of its total dependence on literacy skills. The overhead projector is even worse – at least with a book everyone else is looking down, whereas with an overhead projector people will see that you are not able to follow. The Roman Catholic Church gets neatly round the problem by asking members to learn the service by heart. In the UK one in five adults is unable to read a simple set of instructions,[2] and in an area of deprivation the proportion is bound to be much higher – so associating worship with reading automatically loses a church a quarter of its potential participants.

Prison chapel services can be dire, but I attended one where the female inmates had worked together with their chaplain Janet Allwright to produce their own service. It had just the right ease of access without being childish, and was designed for people with short attention spans who were used to noise and tension around the chapel. The songs, the sermon and the theme were all directly related to the experience of prison life – referring to Jesus' imprisonment and to what freedom could actually mean. It was liturgy which brought solace, challenge and promise – it 'praised open' a confining and depressing situation, and brought new life to the whole prison community.

Some congregational worship died the death years ago and one wishes that a few of the congregation would go and visit other churches for a couple of weeks to experience what they're missing, so that they could take back suggestions to enliven the worship in the home church. I have known all styles of worship to work wonderfully well in the urban setting – high solemn Mass with bells and smells, charismatic hand-waving services, small intimate healing services, mission sing-alongs or traditional Mattins and Evensong – but only if they are presented well, with honesty and care to offer the best that is possible. I have also known slovenly and irresponsible worship, offered by people who should know better. Since the worship of God is the highest form of human endeavour, it deserves our best, but it too can be subject to power tussles where a few hang on to control even though they have no gift for it.

Sometimes the small intimate group can be very appropriate for newcomers to the faith, for it can offer the security required to open oneself up to the presence of God. Here there can be an attractive visual focus for worship and the assurance of friends to assist if emotions are difficult to handle. There is an abundance of material now available on CD and in picture form, as well as candles, draperies and so on, all designed to help worship to be the meaningful challenge that it should be. Although searchers can be helped to connect with their deeper emotions and questions in small intimate groups of this sort, they may then find that the larger gathering is either helpfully anonymous or else fails to have the same personal impact or accessibility for them. It will depend upon individual temperament. We must remember that many people need help if they are to gain most from communal worship, so introductory sessions, and perhaps a mentor to help them through services to begin with, can prove helpful.

The church that takes care with its worship, and with how people share in it, finds that good, appropriate liturgy can be a springboard to insightful reflection and action for the groups and individuals who experience it. It is a place where we see the Kingdom vision, so that all our action can be judged by it, and where we can be empowered to live out the vision in our lives.

Engaged listening

In addition to our congregational worship, house groups, cell groups, Bible groups, study courses and the like, can all help in the continuing work of nurturing members in the faith. Many colleges and denominations offer courses of study where lay people and clergy together can learn more about their faith and its great treasures. Congregational ministers must see it as their prime responsibility to know the traditions of Bible, liturgy, Church history, doctrine, hymnody, and so on, if they are to resource their people in Christian reflection on community issues. If, however, they do not have the gift for this themselves, they must make sure that those who do are well resourced and able to help the congregation shape its mission by listening for God's perspective amid all the clamour of the urban scene. When the stories we have gathered from the community are broken open, we expect the light of our Christian traditions to flood in and resonate with the issues, so it will be very important that those Christian treasures are known about and readily available for that purpose within the congregation or group.

Jesus did not choose to enter into his ministry in a formal way until he had lived in the community, experiencing its travails and its joys for something like thirty years – a very long time in the life of a first-century person. During this time he was no doubt observing and reflecting, listening and questioning, and we must do the same. He would have met a wide variety of people in his profession and gained great insights into how his society functioned and managed its affairs, determined its political life and conducted its religious observance. Only then did he venture upon his public ministry. This is reason enough for us to take great care in observing and analysing our own situation if we are to impact it in any effective manner.

Social analysis

Care must be taken by the church as it gathers the stories and information about the neighbourhood and its issues, that it does not fall into the trap of believing that one can be thoroughly objective about these things – or even that one should be. We are expecting of the urban church a prophetic stance of critical engagement, not critical distancing. To learn that one-third of all children in the UK are living below the government's designated poverty line could not possibly leave a person dispassionate or totally objective! That is why, once the information is gathered, then careful analysis is called for, in order to create as true a picture as possible.

The group may not of course be operating within a parish or locality, and the object of its concern may be its members' shared interest, their workplace, or a political issue. The group may have a single issue upon which they choose to focus, perhaps looking at international trade, transport issues, finance, urban health, education, or something of that sort. The group may have a particular constituency – all elderly or young, or maybe all architects or financiers searching from within their own experience for a Kingdom way to live and work. We assume that such groups can meet together, but it may be that they will rely upon the telephone and computer technology to bring them together over distances. Whatever the object of their concern, the stories, data and information need to be gathered and analysed, and there will usually be resources to help them in that.

In the parish setting, a group needs to be formed to undertake a full exploration of the locality and to share the stories about what makes the community tick. After that anecdotal phase, it moves into more careful analysis of the matter, teasing out the issues and collecting hard data. Maps and newspapers all help the group to balance the felt experiences of the community with the statistical information, so that a clearer and more accurate picture begins to emerge. They will need to know the needs and strengths of the area, who the key players of the community are, where the prime institutions are located and what they do, and what the dominant values of the locality might be. Work sheets have been published to help us to undertake this task, and I have also written it up in some detail in *Let's Do Theology*. In that book I explain how an area can be analysed by ordinary local people but in quite strategic ways, looking at the historical, geographical, social, economic, cultural and religious factors which make any community tick. This exercise usually proves to be great fun, and can result in intense interest being shown by church and non-church people alike who are committed to the area. It is easy to log on to the government website at <www.statistics.gov.uk/neighbourhood/> and type in the local postcodes to see the most recent census data clearly set out. The local library and diocesan office can also offer statistical information to help build up the local picture, while the local authority is usually able to direct the group towards some of the issues which they believe to be key. It's good during this exercise to visit other churches and groups, both voluntary and statutory, who have a stake in the community, so that their perspectives can also be gleaned. Eventually a fine analysis of the community can result, comprising written, photographic and even recorded materials. At this point some groups have an open day where all the locals are invited to see the pictures, press cuttings, statistics, postcards and so on, and that helps everyone celebrate the community they belong to.

At the same time we do well to find out how our own church presence is seen by the community, and Benny Hazlehurst and Chris Chapman have produced a wonderful 'do it yourself' *Kit* for housing estate churches[3] in which they suggest we stand opposite our church building and ask, 'What does the building say to the community about the Christian faith?' For those who feel intimidated, does it intimidate even further? Does the look of the building and its surroundings convince busy, rushed people passing by that this is a place where they will sense God's presence in their lives? Does it tell people what to expect if they come along, and can they assume that their personal needs will be catered for here? If we are very honest, we have to be ready for some worrying answers.

As the Christian group goes about this attentive listening, getting the information together and building the picture of the community, it is vital that they try to draw out what the dominant values of the area might be. Joe Hasler[4] in Bristol is keen that the Church listens to deeply working-class cultures, bidding us attend to what is being said amid the language codes and lifestyles, to see how the matriarchal societal structures, street cultures and workplace attitudes all signify the values the community espouses. What Joe is doing is reminding us that underneath all the data and the stories we collect will be lurking values and systems of meaning which will be crucial for us to understand as urban missioners. As we collect the information together, we must therefore look for connections and patterns, so that we discern what these underlying values might be, and so better understand the causes of the griefs and joys of the people with whom we are living.

But a note of caution. When I was at St Chad's parish in Birmingham, our poor estate was forever being surveyed by one government department or another. Research students too were constantly knocking on doors or sending round surveys. Eventually it became something of a community sport to make up outrageous responses just to see the expressions on the faces of the surveyors. What that did to the official statistics for our area I dread to think. That same community responded so differently, I'm glad to say, when we did our own parish audit, and I think that was because it was undertaken by people like themselves who, being locals, were already known and trusted. But another word of warning too. It is all too easy to assume we understand a culture when we don't. In my youth, when my sister first brought home her husband-to-be, our parents were quite concerned that he had what, to them, was a distinctly Plaistow accent. They saw Plaistow as another world – and yet it was only a ten-minute bus ride away, and I suspect a non-cockney could never distinguish the difference in . accent. We must never underestimate just how complex cultures are, nor our need to listen to those others who we may think we already understand.

It certainly makes a difference that Anglican clergy are legally bound to live in the midst of the communities they serve. It brings them much closer to the reality as they share personally in the joys and worries of the place, rather than looking on from outside. Of course, being at one with the community is not as easy for the vicar as it once was. Simply visiting parishioners can now constitute a major problem. High-rise tenements and terraces may now sport steel-plated doors and elaborate security systems, and the most vulnerable are loath to open the door to anyone at all. I have found that carrying a clip-board is more likely to get you past the security than a dog collar! Walking and travelling by public transport puts us in touch with local people on a day-to-day basis, and then we can rely on the telephone for the deeper pastoral conversations. Two golden rules that I have seen broken at great cost are, first, never communicate by memo; and second, always check first whether shaking hands is a sign of friendship or of suited officialdom. Living observantly in the community soon alerts one to the finer points.

Some community realities soon come home to resident clergy. 'Redlining' is that despicable practice whereby insurance and other financial agencies refuse to offer their services to anyone living within certain high-risk postcode areas. With no insurance cover available, residents, including the vicar, become more vulnerable to burglary and theft, and if loans are needed they have to be negotiated with the loan shark. I must say, however, that one particular insurance company must be commended, for when Nihal Paul informed them that his church hall had been stolen they could not quite believe it – contents yes, but surely not the whole building? Although they were somewhat amazed by the extravagance of the crime, and the policy certainly did not cover such an eventuality, they did offer at least a little financial compensation.

Feeling the same stresses and strains as our parishioners is essential to understanding something of the reality of the community's experience. I remember how angry I felt that the developers of the London Docklands did not care about the pollution they were causing locally, or the fact that their buildings were preventing TV signals reaching local homes. These were not simply interesting stories for me, because I was coughing with everybody else, and my family could not watch their favourite programmes either. You cannot beat living in the community, and this is often why the clergy really do know how the community feels about their area and are among the first to be involved in community action.

However, even though we live our lives so close to the community, clergy will never really know the full experience of being constrained to live for ever in bad places. We can always ask for a transfer or maybe even go for a refreshing holiday. Others have never had a break away in their lives. Similarly, just recently I attended a gathering at a local Roman Catholic church where a troop of Muslim dancers from the former Yugoslavia were sharing their traditional songs and dances and telling us their stories. There is no way that any of us could begin to appreciate the horror which these people had experienced. Seeing their children and parents butchered and then making the fearful journey to safety in Britain is not, please God, ever going to be part of our own life story. And yet these and other asylum-seekers are part of our community and are helping to shape its present and future values. So while we must always become one with our communities as much as possible, we must also reserve the right of others to tell us how differently it feels for them.

Building the networks

Once we have performed our parish audit or looked thoroughly and analytically at the particular issue concerning our group, the listening must not stop there. Very often an urban church may be so small in numbers that it can only build up a sufficient critical mass if it links up with other local and interested people. We have already mentioned the importance of working very closely with other Christian denominations, but we have increasing opportunities in Britain today to include the insights of other faith communities too.

A further step in attaining this holistic vision can be for the local congregation to connect with other congregations further afield. Some have created links between inner-city and suburban parishes to the mutual advantage of both. They have learnt how the problems they each face are symptoms of much larger issues which they can address together. Sometimes however, old patronizing attitudes mar the link and little is learnt, so to help spot these pitfalls the Baptist Union has written a spoof letter to highlight the problems.

Dear Friends at Poorchurch,

I expect you are surprised to get a letter from us, a wealthy congregation at the Much Blessing Baptist Church. When our treasurer told us about you we were appalled! Such poverty! It must be awful for you. We have an old duplicator you might be able to use. I think it still works but you may need to have it serviced. You need help with your Mission forms so our Mrs Phillips will do them for you. She wouldn't be able to come to your neighbourhood because she's just bought a new car, so send them over. Our treasurer tells us that you are having lots of windows broken. Have you thought of just boarding them up? I'm sure you'd feel patronized if we offered you money so we won't do that but be assured of our prayers . . .

. . . and so on. Suffice it to say that links of this sort have to be handled very sensitively indeed.

Helpful links can also be made between rural and urban churches. The Cathedral of St John the Divine in New York set up a special meeting to encourage some twenty community leaders drawn from both rural and urban districts to share their experiences and learn from each other. Clearly the dimensions of the problems they faced were on different scales, but the interconnectedness of the issues became very evident. In Britain we find that many of the new arrivals into the UK from Africa, Asia and Eastern Europe hail from very rural backgrounds and I have found it fascinating to bring them into conversation with our own rural communities to discuss how the European Common Agricultural Policy has impoverished both communities.

Just as our rural and urban communities rarely have a chance to meet, similarly the segregation of urban dwellers one from another by the quartering and zoning which we have described makes it difficult for urban people to understand how similar issues affect people in other urban zones. As a bishop, I find myself meeting people from all walks of life and I am amazed by the fact that so many have no notion of, nor any opportunity to find out, how people who live close by but in a different social grouping live their lives. Our mutual ignorance is extraordinary. The Church is often one organization which reaches across those barriers and can enable sharing to take place.

But we can also learn about the ramifications of our local issues by looking even further afield. We can attend Christian Aid functions, or read books and papers such as the *New Internationalist* magazine which produces very manageable data in pictorial form, and begin to discern how our local issues relate us to others across the globe. But there is no substitute for real meeting with people who can share their international experience – and the city is the place where that can easily happen. Christians Aware too has been enabling ordinary Christian people to meet across the continents for many years.

A great deal of research has recently been undertaken within the discipline of urban studies which helps us to see the international background against which so much of our mission is now taking place. It must be acknowledged however that not all that material is in accessible form, and so a group may find it easier to read the books that Andrew Davey and I have produced as introductions to the subject.[5] In this way the group will see even more clearly how their own concerns link to causes which are altogether outside their immediate community.

Some Christian groups may find it difficult to be as inclusive as I am suggesting. We are being told by some within the Church Growth movement for example that congregations grow fastest when they target their evangelism specifically at only one cultural group, whereas I am arguing for the inclusion of a diverse mixture – which may well therefore have adverse consequences for growth in congregational size. I am convinced however that size is not all; there is also a tremendous need for congregations to be true to the Kingdom mind-set, and a significant feature of the Kingdom banquet is that we will find ourselves sitting next to people who we thought should not belong there. We will all find it difficult to be as inclusive as Christ demands because all human beings wrestle with an innate tribalism which, at its worst, demonizes the other and assumes a personal superiority over them. Even the New Testament Church slipped repeatedly from the ideal. But the Kingdom calls for a repentant and welcoming spirituality and that will empower us to become more open to the new urban world and the challenge of our cosmopolitan mission.

Choosing our partners

The United Nations tells us that there is a global shift in how town and city leaders across the world view themselves.[6] They have moved 'from managerialism to entrepreneurialism', viewing their town or city 'as a product that needs to be marketed so that it appeals to global investors'. They now think of themselves less as service providers and more as the overseers of others' investment. The political process of urban regeneration therefore now comprises four steps:

1. Partnerships, where local groups are encouraged to devise solutions together to their problems;
2. Leverage, where public money is used to attract private investment and resources to enact those solutions;
3. Competition, where the 'best' solutions are allowed to attract the most investment;
4. Results, where 'outputs', such as jobs created, houses built, and so on, are the expected criteria for assessment, rather than simply judging a policy on how much money was expended upon it.

This means that before funding is available, the local community must be seen to be acting together in some sort of 'partnership', and into that partnership mix come such players as developers, financiers, local voluntary groups and the local authority, and of course the local church.

At their best, partnerships should be a sign of our common bond of concern for the well-being of our community. Unfortunately this has rarely turned out to be the case in urban regeneration schemes, and indeed 'partnership' was recently defined by one experienced cynic as 'the suspension of mutual loathing in pursuit of money'. Urban places are almost by definition highly contested places, and so the creation of trusting partnership schemes has to take place across chasms of cultural and social mistrust that may have been deepening for years. Good, sustainable partnerships in these circumstances are only possible if they have a rare spiritual depth and integrity – but miracles do happen!

It may feel rather flattering to be asked to be a partner in some grand scheme for the community if we are but a small congregation struggling to find our way, but we must nevertheless keep our wits about us. It may be that the proposals are somewhat lacking and the Church is being brought into the partnership only in order to give a stamp of legitimacy to the undertaking. All too often it is only when the bigger picture is understood or the details of the plan become clear that we begin to see the weakness or even the immorality of a local scheme. Much of the housing stock of the East End of London is being redeveloped or gentrified in order, it is said, to create a more balanced mix of social and private housing, but we may therefore wonder why the same social mix is never talked about with regard to the wealthy reaches of housing in the West End of London. As the population of the East End is decanted into poorer housing to make way for the new developments, so the overall quantity of social housing is reduced and the developers reap the benefits of the increase in land values. A local church group may feel that at their level it all looks just fine, and they sign up to the partnership, never realizing what they have thereby given legitimacy to.

The Agape Café had been successfully run by St Mary's, Willesden, as a centre for the homeless, but when the new partnership saw the introduction of professional workers, the criteria for entry to the centre changed radically. The vicar began noticing rough sleepers who had once been regular attenders at the Café now out on the street again, and so started up a new, and this time independent, night shelter open to all without strings. They have now created a 'community of friends' with the homeless, and left the partnership to its own devices.

Sometimes it can be even worse than that. Roger Driver reports that in the area of Bootle where he lives as vicar, there are no fewer than seventy-five separate government initiatives all designed to hit, or 'target', the same poor people, and which bring in professional workers on very short-term contracts who therefore disable the locals. One health worker responded to his question about consultation, 'We did try that but the people said they didn't want what we were offering, so we haven't done that again.' Roger keeps advising us that the only way for these partnerships to work is to 'start small and build slow'.

Winning funds is still not easy, and although the mantra is that the proposals must come from the locals, all too often they are later turned down because they don't conform to central criteria. We find that the literacy and professionalism required to make a successful bid for funds precludes the fullest participation of any but those who know the system. Often it is way beyond the capacities of poor people, even if they had the will to undertake the task. This means that it is usually left to a few able locals to make all the running, and there is really little telling whether they are representative of the community or not.

It is interesting to note that the partnership programmes all seem to be directed towards addressing people who are needy and excluded, rather than challenging those who are rich and who manage the systems of exclusion. The implication seems to be that by challenging the poor and excluded, the system which excludes them can be ignored and everything will come right. The rules of the game seem to be managed from the perspective and for the benefit of the powerful, and sometimes run counter to our gospel mandates.

Having pointed out some of the pitfalls of the government programmes, we must nevertheless be thankful that we have a government which really wants to work hard to get it right for the poor communities of our land. Much of what the Urban White Paper 2000 promised is very much in line with the hopes that the Church had been voicing for many years, and our national leaders are to be commended. Our concerns are more about the interpretations of policy and the standards of delivery we are experiencing at more local levels. My hope is therefore that despite the problems, urban ministers and congregations will continue to work in partnerships wherever the Kingdom promise is being glimpsed, while careful, ongoing theological reflection should keep us alert to the pitfalls and inevitable limitations. Choosing partners is never an easy decision, but perhaps going in with our eyes open, determined to be treated not merely as cheap service providers but as critical partners, offers us the hope of doing our best rather than doing nothing.

For all our necessary reticence, the signs are that it can be quite wonderful when the partnerships work and when we find ways to put the management of community issues into the hands of representative local groups. And we have examples all around the country where this seems genuinely to be happening. The New Deal for Communities project at Earlham and Marlpit in Norwich has been well documented,[7] and the priest, Sam Wells, attests that the regeneration there is growing out of the experience of the poor, rather than the assumptions of the rich. A group of local people have given their all to driving the development, which has been based upon the investment of very large sums of money, but this 'throwing money at the problem' has in turn 'started a remarkable debate about what is good in the locality, and what is bad; what should grow and what should wither'. Similarly, the Vange Estate in Basildon has been the recipient of funding which has been spent on upgrading the housing stock and enabling the local community to elect its own governing body. The game is one of constantly changing goal-posts, waltzing round with partners in order to find match-funding, and all the time trying to see the issues through the plethora of minute detail. The urban minister needs to juggle all these skills if she or he is to play the 'Regeneration Game'. But despite all the headaches, says David the local priest, the community is benefiting wonderfully from their partnership scheme.

This brief discussion of the benefits and pitfalls of joining government partnerships only arose however in relation to our prime concern, which is to argue for the importance of working with others where possible, as we seek to listen attentively to all those who have a stake in our community. This multi-disciplinary and multi-agency approach helps us to think more creatively about the issues that we seek to address, recognizing that our community is but one part of a global, complex dynamic. We can learn the same lesson from George Barlow, the Chief Executive of the Peabody Trust which provides social housing in London. He writes, 'Housing Association schemes must be diverse and innovative, recognising the interconnections between housing, employment, education, training and community development. Providing good quality, affordable housing is only one piece of a complex jigsaw.'[8] Christian urban ministry groups must have the same holistic attitude about their missionary endeavours, while retaining as their anchor the Gospel principles of the Kingdom of God.

Bringing it all together

Having listened attentively to the community in which it is set or to the issue with which it is concerned, the Christian congregation or group will have gathered stories, information and data and taken time to analyse and focus the issues and the underlying values which emerge. They will have worked with others in the field, learning from their different perspectives, and sharing in project partnerships where appropriate. However, all this listening and analysing will not have been undertaken for its own sake, but for the sole purpose of helping to better our Christian witness and urban mission. To this end, the group will have immersed itself all the while in prayer and worship, 'praising open' the situation, and comparing all that it has found from its surveys and audit with the Christian story and the Kingdom principles.

Again, for a detailed description of how this theological reflection may be done to best effect I would direct the reader to my *Let's Do Theology*, but suffice it here to say that it can prove to be a very enjoyable and exciting exercise, especially when undertaken by a mix of people of all ages and all social and educational backgrounds. It begins, as we shall see, with spotting the connections and disconnections between our own situation and the story of Jesus.

CURBS is a project for 'Children in Urban Situations' which works with children's spirituality and children's issues, rather than from a skill-based approach. As the issues which concern the children become clear, so the stories of Bible and faith resonate with their own experiences and they are helped to make the links for themselves. Again, working with adults in Advent, a number of Churches in London's Docklands produced worksheets for local groups to study, which helped people to make the connections between the issues they were facing and the stories of the

Christian gospel. Each weekly work-sheet concentrated on an issue which had come from the groups themselves – 'Homes', 'Land, money and power', 'Values in the city', and so on – and presented each issue in an exciting and accessible way. At the end of each week of biblical reflection on an issue, government ministers, developers and national faith leaders were invited to come to an open seminar at Poplar parish church where they had to face the tough questions from the community which had come to light during the Bible study sessions. The meetings were lively, to say the least!

Daybreak is a Christian drug project which is well versed in helping people come to terms with their deeper spiritual needs as they seek to address their addiction. They have learnt to use a very non-directive approach, which allows addicts to make their own spiritual journey, giving them space to make their own connections with the spiritual treasures that are there for them, and which relate to their predicament.

Unlock is the training organization which was originally called the Evangelical Urban Training Project (EUTP). Its former co-ordinator, Jenny Richardson, has been holding seminars and workshops up and down the country for years, helping urban people who perhaps do not have the skills or inclination to read books, to find and express their Christian faith in powerful ways. The process is the same again – the group works out what the key issues are for the neighbourhood, and then looks to the stories of the Bible and other Christian traditions to see the connections. Finally they work out ways in which they can so live and act together that they enable those biblical dynamics to be experienced again in their own community. Sometimes of course the group will not feel that they know the Bible sufficiently well, but they will have prayers that they know by heart, they will have seen videos, know hymns, be able to tell the stories of the saints, or whatever else, so that they can help to make the connections which are instrumental to theological reflection. Many organizations have published excellent introductions to Bible, Church, and other Christian basics, which provide new Christians with basic faith information. What will turn the group into a theologically reflective group, however, will be the quality of the connections they can make between those treasures of the faith and the issues that have been raised as they have studied their community. It is from those connections that the vision will begin to form as to what might be the Kingdom action to take in their situation.

I was once involved with a church project which had been a long time in the planning, but soon after it opened its doors, it ran into problems. It reminded Fred, one of the group members, of how Jesus, soon after his baptism, was taken aside by the power of the Holy Spirit to think his ministry through and be tempted to undertake it in different ways. His first temptation was to turn stones into bread to save himself. His reply was, 'We do not live on bread alone.' From that, Beryl made the connection and realized how easy it would be for our project to produce short-term solutions, and ignore the deeper underlying issues – 'every word that issues from God's mouth'. Next Jesus was tempted to throw himself down from a high place and show the crowds that he was unhurt. The equivalent temptation for us was to undertake the project in order to claim attention and kudos for ourselves rather than attend to the needs of those for whom the project existed. Third, Jesus was offered domination of all the world if only he would worship the devil. Go along with the powers that be without question, and in that way gain the funding! Having made these three connections between our project and the Bible story, we were then better prepared to face the work from a Kingdom of God perspective than we would have been had we met with success straight away.

The vision emerges

In each of the foregoing examples the dynamic has been the same – the stories of our situation and experience are connected with the stories of the faith – and, as the connections are made, so the Holy Spirit breathes into the Christian group a vision for the work that lies ahead.

So often, when we make bids for funding, we are made to emphasize the weaknesses and the deprivation of a community, but it is much better to work from the light that God shines onto a situation than from the darkness that reduces our hopes and expectations. This is why our listening process has to be attentive to what people have to offer and not just to the problems they confront. Seeing children singing together with great glee and exuberance was the vision that inspired the Kingsland Youth Choir. All the children come from poor and deprived homes but the vision for the choir did not start with those problems – it started from a conviction that within each child is the voice of freedom. Another fine project originated from the positive vision that God gives us 'love on a plate'. The Haven Restaurant in Glasgow now serves up meals which bring people together in a warm and supportive atmosphere without strings attached. Surrounding the restaurant are day-care facilities, advice and information boards, educational meetings and a group that works with victims of trauma and torture.

A sense of awe is the root of vision. For some, the vision will be written in grand terms – affordable housing, accessible public transport, quality services, community cohesion, security, and so on. For others, the vision may resonate with the famous 'Isaiah Vision' in Isaiah 65, of a community where children are well cared for, old people live in dignity, people build houses and live in them, and those who plant vineyards eat the fruit. The important thing is that the group finds a vision that it can really call its own, for out of that vision, action will be fashioned. It may be that the outcomes will seem minimal when compared with what other, more 'successful' churches achieve, but Jesus warns us not to see it this way. He speaks of a mustard seed, which although only tiny has something of Kingdom mystery about it so that it gently grows, to such an extent that eventually everyone finds themselves nesting in its branches.

Faithful action

Having seen the connections forming between the community issues and the stories of faith and Bible, the vision forms and the ideas for action percolate up. I use the word 'action' somewhat guardedly however, for I do not want to give the impression that the only outcomes of this process are the setting up of grand schemes and projects – far from it. It may be that the outcome of the exercise, even after many months of hard work, is a decision simply to talk more with our neighbours, or form a prayer cell. On the other hand, however small may be the outcome, it must not be insignificant – it must 'signify' something greater than itself if it is to be true to the model of Jesus' ministry. Each of his actions pointed to an aspect of the Kingdom and spoke volumes about it; in this sense, it was a sacramental action. Our actions should seek to do the same. We might set up a local debt-counselling centre or a credit union, which can remind us of the way in which debt holds people in thrall around the globe, and of the mutual forgiveness which is God's Kingdom gift to us. A 'bring and buy' club can open up all the issues of recycling and waste accumulation and point to the need to be better stewards of God's creation. We may campaign for better town governance, for more accessible public spaces, or for a re-think about gentrification and gated communities in the locality, in order that it may become a place 'for the many not just the few'. Whatever our projects, they must be managed and presented with these deeper meanings to the fore.

Sometimes a group's vision will prompt it simply to share with others what it has learnt from its process of attentive listening. The Poverty Hearings which have been held up and down the country issued from a vision that if only people in authority could hear first hand the stories of those who suffer poverty, then all sorts of things could follow. Others have found that getting involved with Christian Aid debt campaigning, or homelessness education, has been the way they can best express their awareness of the Kingdom, and so have disseminated diagrams, booklets and other information resources far and wide. Other groups have gone further and engaged in campaigns that have brought important matters of injustice or deprivation to the attention of others. Fair-traded goods have been introduced onto the counters of local supermarkets, asylum-seekers have had opportunities to explain their experiences and cultures to others, public health issues have been paraded in marketplaces, campaigning leaflets distributed and people informed. This sort of activity engages local people in their strength and puts otherwise vulnerable people in the driving seat, so that they develop their skills and self-confidence while engaging the 'powers and principalities' on a Kingdom issue.

To undertake activities of this sort the group has to learn how to organize events, manage people, campaign and lobby, raise the funds, evaluate and monitor, as they go. There are courses on offer now across the country, and very often training days are provided by organizations where church groups are welcome to attend. Each issue of the ecumenical *Urban Bulletin* lists a wealth of such training opportunities.

Maybe it is a matter of temperament, but other Christian groups will prefer to become involved directly in helping and caring in the community. There is certainly something very rewarding about being in a practical project or club which is modelled on Kingdom principles. Keith, a biker and notorious drugs dealer, came to Christ and wanted to respond in a hands-on manner by sharing his new-found joy with others. He set about gathering old bikes and with a few friends set up a small workshop in which he shared his mechanical skills with youngsters off the streets who wanted to ride their bikes with more skill and care. So 'Youth-Bike' was formed from his knowledge of the locality and the evident need of local youngsters. The whole atmosphere of the club speaks volumes about the empowering of the Spirit and the change that the Kingdom of God brings to the lives of those who are touched by it.

The arts can play a very important part in Kingdom living and activity. The Ascension Eagles is an enormous club of youngsters in the East End of London who are trained, and train each other, in the American style, as cheerleaders. They dance and move to the music, wave their pom-poms and perform all sorts of acrobatics with great enthusiasm, to the roar of the crowd and the pride of their parents. The church to which they belong expects each member to care for other members of the club, to support one another and retain a friendly attitude while in the club – and from then on, it's all fun! In Basildon, after the horrific events in New York on 11 September 2001, the mosque was attacked and local Asian women were abused in the street. As a consequence local faith leaders staged a community day with speakers, performed wonderful Indian and African dance, set up a market of stalls run by various cultural groups, and offered good free food from around the world. It was living evidence that God can bring wonderful togetherness out of the most horrific terror.

Some church groups may not be able, for one reason or another, to create gestures on such a grand scale, but all can respond to their vision in some way. Brightening their worship and making their prayers more alert to the needs of the community, opening up their building a little more, putting their hall at the disposal of local clubs, or whatever it may be – all these things can play their small part in welcoming in the Kingdom. But in all this, one thing is paramount. There should always be somewhere in the background, if not overtly, a very clear intention that everything that is done should be an attempt to relate the gospel to the community. I would hope that in each and every church there could be a group, perhaps even the Church Council itself, whose major purpose is to make sure that every-thing that is done in that church makes sense in terms of the Kingdom principles. I once had the joy of helping to run a Community Advice Centre from a little back-street church where I was the vicar. Its glory was the fact that every fortnight a group of those involved would meet as the 'Parables in Action' group, to discuss how everything was going, reflect upon that with their Bibles open on their laps, and help to frame the Centre's policy for the weeks ahead. In this way the Advice Centre became a learning experience for all and a source of theological insight and faithful action.

Whether our projects are small and easily managed or whether they become key to the regeneration of the whole locality, if all is geared to the Kingdom principles it will be a tremendously empowering experience, allowing those who live it, to have a foretaste of the Kingdom, 'on earth as it is in heaven'. We sense we are participating in something of real worth because the project not only assists and empowers at a local level, but par-ticipates in an issue of global significance. InterAct has set up a computer exchange which upgrades old PCs and sends them to African church employment projects. The Time Exchange at West Bromwich Baptist Church has enlarged the normal helping network of the congregation to the whole community. People offer their time and skill to neighbours on a points basis and exchange their points for help from others. The scheme helps the long-term unemployed to prepare themselves for the routines of work once again, builds self-esteem, unites the community, and at the same time challenges the global market by reconnecting the economics of currency exchange with human skill and community building.

Mission and evangelism

If all our Christian projects and programmes are underpinned by theological reflection as I have suggested, this puts an end to the unhelpful separation of evangelism from social action. If our care for the needy is divorced from our worship and theological reflection, both suffer immeasurably. I was once showing a priest around the parish I was serving, and took him into a pub to meet a number of locals. As we sat round the table enjoying our pints, the priest got a good quizzing. Johnny asked my visitor exactly what he did. The priest tried to explain that his interest was in empowering urban people through the methods of Community Organizing. He went on at length until one listener interposed, 'You haven't mentioned God yet, but if you're with him (pointing to me) my bet is that you're from the Church.' 'Well, yes actually, I'm a priest,' replied my friend. From then on the locals did not want to listen any more and broke off the conversation and went and played snooker. The next day I saw them again and asked why they'd stopped the conversation, and was interested to hear that it wasn't because my friend had been religious but, as they put it, 'He didn't have the bottle to come clean in the first place.' Urban people like to know what they're getting and don't respect a person who won't own up to their beliefs and their faith – but if we do, they'll deal with that and take it from there. The Church understands the five marks of mission to include both evangelism and caring for the needy, caring for creation, addressing the unjust structures of society and nurturing Christian disciples. The complete change of life which the Kingdom of God calls for involves preaching the Good News of Jesus in both word and action, not as separated activities but as one saving grace. Undertaking that task by way of the method I have described will address the fact that while people have clearly given up coming to church, there is no reason why the Church cannot come to them – and come to them right at the heart of the issues that really do concern them in their communities. We have always preached that Jesus is the answer, but my plea is that we stop first to listen to what the question might be. In this way, people will know that the Kingdom truly is the answer – it scratches where they itch.

Celebrating the Kingdom

Kingdom action should begin and end, like the Lord's Prayer, with praise, awe and the celebration of God. I have often told the story of a very depleted group of elderly women who had for many years been knitting items in support of Leprosy Mission. I was intrigued to learn from them something of the complexity of their handicraft. They showed me that sometimes knitting can be a relaxed and spontaneous exercise, but on other occasions it is intricate and demanding as the patterns become more complex and involved. We reflected that most creativity is of that dual quality. We then turned to the book of Genesis to see what light it could throw on this issue of creativity. The group were intrigued to find there two stories of creation, one story of extravagant spontaneity on God's part, and the other of an ordered and patterned daily procedure. So it was that the Bible stories chimed in with all that the women knew about creativity from the knitting they had been doing all their lives. Next we learnt about leprosy and saw that the stories recorded in the Bible define the disease as a cause for separation and segregation. As we reflected upon the records of Jesus' healings, so we recognized that he brought the lepers back into relationship once again with the whole body of the community. Just as the women knew that if one woollen stitch were severed, the whole garment would unravel, so the healing stories were reminding them that if one person is cut off, then community itself disintegrates. Even their own group was coming apart because some were now too old to attend and were probably sitting at home, forgotten and isolated. Like the lepers, they were segregated and separated, and were desperate for community healing. At the end of this process, one Sunday evening the church was turned over to a celebration of all that had been learnt. Bible readings from the Creation stories were followed by a demonstration of knitting, and all the congregation were allowed to try their hand. Next, the story of Jesus' healing of the ten lepers was read, and the international work of Leprosy Mission was described. It was then explained that when Jesus heals he brings people back into community, and we all applauded to see that those house-bound members of the knitting group who could manage it had been brought back to church that evening for the first time in ages. From now on, members of the congregation who had cars were going to ferry wool to their homes, so they would be included once again in the knitting group. The service was a really joyous occasion. It was all so simple, but so moving and genuinely a celebration of the creativity of God's Kingdom in the midst of our privatized and fragmented community.

Celebratory worship is a thanksgiving for the fact that the powers are unmasked and that we are given opportunities for freedom and empowerment. It includes the 'left-behind ones' and helps the élite to see sense. It is a healing activity and is an honouring of the God who makes it all possible. It reminds the urban community that although it experiences glimpses of the Kingdom in the here and now, the Kingdom is still 'not yet'. However, celebratory worship also reminds the community that in their own life together, they have seen the gap between the 'not yet' and the 'now' closed up just that little bit more.

10 | Wider Horizons

In this book, our prime focus has been upon the work of the local group or congregation, and their minister. But our subject matter warrants a short postscript about the implications for those who work at other levels of the Church. It is essential that those at the coal-face are properly supported by their denominations, and those denominations also have distinctive responsibilities of their own to perform.

First, those of us who see theology as contextual acknowledge that when we gather from our various situations as contextual theologians, we rejoice to find ourselves among kindred spirits. Whether we issue from the ranks of black theology, feminist theology, rural theology, urban theology, or any other clearly contextual framework, we realize that we are nevertheless at one with those from other situations – at one with the 'flow' of what we might call a 'catholic contextual theology'. It is that 'many-voiced' gospel which we described earlier, and which, when heard from those diverse backgrounds, flows together into one. As at Pentecost, we each hear the same Good News in our own language. The wider Church has a responsibility to gather Christians from the various disciplines so that they can sense the excitement of that contextual catholicity.

Second, Jesus addressed the big issues, and to do the same today a multi-levelled approach is ideal. The nation must be addressed at every level and international links fostered. In all this, the denominations can follow our fourfold theological model of listening to the stories, analysing the data, reflection on that in the light of the gospel, and finally, actively responding in mission. In this way, all actions are undertaken from a firm theological rationale. In what follows, we will adopt this fourfold approach, so that we can see once again how it actually works.

But before we do that, let me sound a note of caution. If society is going to listen to the Church today, the institutional Church must first lose its arrogance. It has been too fond of holding itself up as a shining example of Godly living and as a foretaste of heaven, when in fact it can often be well behind society in matters of simple justice and morality. The Church is, however, the privileged instrument of the Kingdom and should glory in its service to that Kingdom rather than concern itself with its own importance. This will be a 'new way of being Church' which perhaps will win back the respect of society, a respect which it has understandably lost in recent years.

So, as with the whole of this book, let us base what follows on that fourfold model of theology which serves the Kingdom style so well.

1. Listening to the local stories

We hear parishes telling us how top-heavy our institutional Church has become. With fewer resources we are trying to sustain a bureaucratic style that grew up when there were people and money enough to manage it, but now the resultant weight of administration keeps clergy at their desks far too much. The institution is therefore seeking to lighten up, simplify and modernize some of its legislation, and offer flexible resources at more local levels, where it counts. Even so, there remains a cultural distance between the different levels of the Church which hinders its mission. Decisions are often made by denominational committees which owe more to middle-class bias than to a listening theology. On one occasion I had just completed researching the importance to the working class of its distinctive cemetery culture when, ironically, the diocesan chancellor imposed conformist strictures upon our churchyards in the interests of what she thought to be 'good taste'. Perhaps it is because of this class bias that many in the Church view our urban areas as problems rather than missional opportunities, and relegate urban issues to special items on their agendas when they should be the mainstream of our missionary concern, since nearly 90 per cent of the country's population is urban. This failure to see the positive opportunities of our towns, estates and cities results in bad Church policy, and denies the Church at large the opportunity to learn from its urban experience.

Many clergy serving in tough areas feel very isolated and vulnerable, and the Church at district level must hear this and take it very seriously. It can encourage mentoring and the peer-support that comes from well-managed and resourced local clergy chapters. Ecumenical alliances, teams, co-operatives and local groupings of parishes can give isolated congregations a new sense of confidence and fresh ideas for mission. We must make sure that among our ecumenical links we involve the new and non-denominational urban churches, so that they do not become isolated either, and so that we can learn from them. Over recent years, urban clergy increasingly fear for the safety and well-being of their families, and it is here again that training, monitoring and meetings to share best practice and concern, can all be helpful. I have also sensed recently that while the Church has rightly been emphasizing the important ministry of lay people, it has allowed clergy morale to suffer. The Church must affirm its clergy! Laity need to hear what a '24/7' life our clergy lead, the pressures they face and the extraordinary breadth of skills they possess. If they are prepared to live 'over the shop', work every weekend with minimal resources and take on tough urban assignments, then they should be honoured, not taken for granted. These talented 'street-jugglers' need a round of applause!

Our Church leaders can also play their part in helping central and local government to understand the nature of the Church. Government often refers in policy papers to the 'faith communities' but thinks of us merely as volunteer service delivery agents with cheap resources of personnel and plant to offer. Occasionally they see us as the local voice of the community, so they use us to add a note of authenticity to their programmes. We have to make plain what we really have to offer, but our participation must never be at the expense of our critical, prophetic engagement. Increasingly, however, officials and politicians forget that Christians are among the 'faith communities' and bypass us altogether. Central government is obviously trying to get their relationship with all the faith communities right, but when at the first parliamentary celebration of Eid they served ham sandwiches, it was clear they are on a steep learning curve when it comes to understanding any of us. The Church itself is not as far forward as it needs to be either, and we should be running racism awareness and ethnicity training, especially in those monochrome areas where there is no face-to-face meeting with people of other cultures. Some Christians remain blissfully unaware of their lack of knowledge and of their racism.

Often the wider national Church is able to bring divergent perspectives together and dioceses find themselves crossing the demarcation lines between communities, governmental regions, urban enclaves and professional bodies. The Government Regional Offices, for example, are crucial determiners today of local regeneration funding and policy, but they can become competitive and self-absorbed. We must bring to all those bodies a realization that there is more to regeneration than business interests and physical refurbishment. Regeneration should be about the soul of a community. If the Church works at those various levels, it can then inform its parishes of how regional and local authority strategies will affect local work, and encourage key personnel from the corporate, voluntary and state sectors to be in touch, so that the various policies cohere.

A Church which is listening at the regional or diocesan level can also make sure that voices are being heard that might not otherwise get a seat at the table with the powerful. For example, if it has a place on the Local Strategic Partnership, an interfaith and ecumenical 'listening group' can make sure that a wide range of local faith voices is heard on the Partnership and an agreed faith-based policy formed. The Church at this level can do a great deal of bridge-building, just as the congregations can at local level. Each diocese should know where their key players are across the region and seek out their opinions so that they can all go into the mix.

Urban issues are not dealt with overnight, and experience tells us that it takes about twenty years to track the outcomes of policy change, so the diocese and deanery will do well to keep this perspective in mind, making local appointments and giving support in accordance with more long-term strategic thinking.

2. Analysing the information

In our urban areas there is increasing division and polarization, but the diocesan or district Church can bring people together and build bridges between areas of deprivation and wealth, between suburbs and inner cities, rural and urban, between monocultural and multicultural communities, between age groups, interest groups and occupations. Often high-profile decision-makers will be surprised to hear the authentic voice of the poor, and the poor will find it strange to hear first hand 'how the other half live'. This sharing helps a more realistic picture to emerge. The Church at diocesan level is also well placed to amass statistical data with the help of such technology as the Geographic Information System, and this can then be handed to each parish so as to sharpen its focus on the life of its local neighbourhood.

To support the theological and missional processes in each congregation, the district Church can also provide adult educational programmes and courses of training. The content and style of the training must however be appropriate to each local context and be determined by the needs of the locals. There are also many professionals, teachers, business managers and so on, who live at a distance from deprived urban areas and yet whose work impacts upon those communities and changes the lives of those who live there. We need educational programmes to raise the awareness of such people so they can see the power implications of their work.

Those groups which are work-based or issue-based rather than congregational, need to be owned by the wider Church, and the diocese can help their learning to be fed into the lives of the congregations, and vice versa. Their perspectives are crucial if we are to open up the Church to the world. Each diocese or district should identify their experts, and where there are universities with urban studies specialists they will often find helpful allies there. The network of urban link and project officers in each diocese has proved invaluable in past years and national conferences and networks of that sort help make the connections and check our stories. Urban and industrial mission, social responsibility networks and justice and peace councils, should, with European and global groups, all be in the mix if we are to open up the issues properly. At national level there are forums for debate and negotiation between government and the Churches, and at international level the Anglican Urban Network[1] is able to bring that wider perspective. On the international front however, we must remember that in some countries the Church has bought into the mind-set of global capitalism even more than we have, so careful theological scrutiny will be called for.

3. Theological reflection

From the many followers Jesus had around him, he selected a very mixed group to be his closest disciples, the majority from marginalized social groups with little previous education. The Church's selection and training procedures on the other hand often de-skill those who have no tertiary education or who are from ethnic minority or working-class backgrounds. Despite their evident leadership and organizational skills exhibited at parish and local level, rarely are black Christians for example really encouraged to take their place in the wider structures of the mainstream Church. We should not be surprised at any of this when we look at the institutional racism, sexism and classism of our institutional Churches. Even as a bishop I find myself debilitated at times by the classist nature of some of the gatherings I'm expected to attend. A theological critique of all our Church power relationships is therefore of paramount importance – we should measure the Church's every activity against that of the man who rode a donkey into Jerusalem.

The Church still finds it hard to understand that solidarity is crucial to empowerment, and continues to separate out black and working-class individuals from others of their own culture during their early years of testing and training – the Church is simply not listening to the cultures of its people. Training has to be contextual and appropriate, and there are, up and down the country, urban theological study centres of excellence that could be playing a more prominent role than they do. These training organizations and institutes are often run on a shoe-string and reliant on free time given by local urban specialists and clergy. The Church sometimes leaves urban ministerial training in the hands of those who are at a remove from urban experience, but ordinands need access to good role models from ethnic minority and working-class backgrounds if the Church is to be equipped with sufficient leadership, able to face our urban challenges.

Denominations must accept that the culture of our poor urban areas means that quite successful urban churches may have to operate with small numbers and small incomes. Urban clergy must be supported so that they can live with the tension between these local realities and the financial and structural expectations of their parent church. They need to know it's OK to risk rather than always to play safe, to look for alternative and exciting ways to operate – setting up church in launderettes and restaurants, working with new structures or none. Bob Toan, the Rural Dean of Birkenhead, helpfully refers to all his failed projects as the 'compost heap' which enriches the soil for another sowing. We must welcome worldly weakness when it results in Kingdom growth.

This leads to a whole raft of issues which the national Church has sooner or later to decide upon. Can it afford to deliver a clergy person to each parish, no matter how small its income? Can a rigid parish system respond in any case to an increasingly mobile and commercial society? The wealthier parishes now hold the purse-strings on policy, so imaginative new ways to be the urban Church will have to be found which can win sufficient funding for them, or find other funding sources. The Church at local and district levels should work theologically together to create strategy which both can own. The Church of England has therefore begun, through its Urban Bishops' Panel, a process of listening and reflection to encourage the recommitment of the national Church to an urban vision so that it can better engage these Church structural issues and address government policies in a fight for Kingdom values.

4. Active responses

At local, regional and national levels, the Church must follow through on its theological strategies with responsive actions which are observably appropriate to the urban context in which they are set. If we fail to act ecumenically in this, or are seen constantly to bicker about churchy issues, then the nation will have the impression that either God's concerns are marginal to their lives, or that to find God they should not look to the Church. In fact we do so badly on these two fronts that I am sometimes amazed that people come to church at all. Sometimes a diocese, district or province will go to the other extreme and produce lots of 'helpful' missional programmes which it then superimposes on its local congregations, putting the parishes in danger of dying the death of a thousand initiatives. In all things, a listening, supportive and yet challenging leadership is required.

The national Church should 'read' our towns and cities – the cultural texts of our times – and speak out for those values which are derived from Kingdom of God principles. This will mean, for example, that our urban church schools must have an inclusivity and excellence about them. Schools are often the bastions of community and civility in very tough environments and deserve our strong support. Youth work likewise, so neglected that the Church is now the largest provider of qualified youth workers in Britain, must be encouraged and built up again. We are facing a dire shortage of teachers, social workers and hospital staff and a break-down of urban infrastructure – and about all this God is concerned and the nation worried. The Kingdom principles speak directly to these national crises, and we therefore have a duty to proclaim their message to our nation. We must be engaged with industry, commerce and the world of work just as much as with ministry to residential communities. The distinctive contribution of the Kingdom community must be offered to a society in crisis.

*   *   *

The British urban story is an exciting tale of discovery, diversity and challenge. Recently, many changes have added to an already complex picture. We are now one of the world's most densely populated nations.[2] Much of our industrial base has been stripped away and we are arguably now the most globalized of the post-industrial economies. International migration has produced towns and cities of immense diversity, and yet by the same token we live in a more polarized society than we have ever known. The cultural signs and markers upon which we have in the past relied are being relativized in a global marketplace of privatized opinion and myth.

British urban life can be full of fun and excitement, with new possibilities and challenging experiences waiting for us at every street corner. And yet, while some neighbourhoods are alive with the buzz of youthful vitality, close by we will find left-behind communities of depression and poverty. In today's urban society we are meeting God's delight and God's pain, moment by moment.

I believe that within all this change and challenge the people of the UK, urban by nature and experience, yearn to see a Church which will stand firm for the justice and truth of its founder – a Church that asks the deep questions and addresses the big issues. And if we look carefully we will find in our urban communities churches which are engaging in building bridges across the cultural divides, setting up projects to assist the poor and give the marginalized a voice. We see local churches which may be small, but which are committed to a Kingdom alternative to the selfish culture which increasingly seeks to dominate our lives. It is a Church which seeks to make good citizens, helpful neighbours and critical thinkers of us all. It worships the one true God, and seeks to offer ministry and mission despite its own shortcomings.

My own denomination, the Church of England, is a family of such diversity that we hang together only by the skin of our teeth. Not all our members have what it takes to be Anglican, and quarrel unnecessarily; but to learn to include differences in this way, with all the tensions that entails, is the only way forward for our globalized, urbanized and fragmented society. We must learn to do it in the Church so that our urbanizing world can do it too – or perish.

I believe the Church will keep true to her urban vocation, and fulfil her call to be the privileged instrument of the Kingdom in those challenging places. But to do so, for God and the world's sake, we must be ever more ambitious for the gospel of Christ and its promise of new life for our towns, cities and estates. For, as the letter to the Hebrews says, we are 'looking forward to the well-founded city, whose architect and builder is God'.

Notes

1. Welcome to an Urban Life

1 For more on this period of working-class history, see M. Young and P. Wilmott, *Family and Kinship in East London* (Routledge & Kegan Paul, 1957); Alan Palmer, *The East End – Four Centuries of London Life* (John Murray Ltd, 1989); Kenneth Leech, *Through Our Long Exile: Contextual Theology and the Urban Experience* (Darton, Longman & Todd, 2001).

2 Anne Power, *Property Before People: The Management of Twentieth Century Council Housing* (Allen & Unwin, 1987).

3 Gibson Winter, *The Suburban Captivity of the Church* (Doubleday, 1961).

4 See Laurie Green, 'Blowing Bubbles: Poplar', in *God in the City*, ed. P. Sedgwick (Mowbray, 1995).

5 *Faith and Community: A Good Practice Guide for Local Authorities* (Local Government Association, 2002).

6 D. H. Lawrence, *The Letters of D. H. Lawrence* (Cambridge University Press, 1981).

7 Ebenezer Howard, *Tomorrow: A Peaceful Path to Real Reform* (London, Swan Sonnenschein & Co., 1898).

2. Telling the Urban Story

1 Jürgen Moltmann, 'Theology in the Project of the Modern World', in *A Passion for God's Reign*, ed. Miroslav Volf (Eerdmans, 1998).

2 Richard Batey, *Jesus and the Forgotten City* (Baker, 1991), p. 136.

3 J. A. Overman, 'Who Were the First Urban Christians?: Urbanization in Galilee in the First Century', in *SBL Seminar Papers*, ed. David Lull (Scholars Press, 1988), p. 165.

4 David Bosch, *Transforming Mission: Paradigm Shifts in the Theology of Mission* (Orbis, 1991), p. 130.

5 Robert Jewett, 'Tenement Church and Pauline Love Feasts', in *Paul: The Apostle to America* (John Knox, 1994).

6 Douglas Edwards, 'First Century Urban/Rural Relations in Lower Galilee: Exploring the Archaeological and Literary Evidence', in *SBL Seminar Papers,* ed. David Lull (Scholars Press, 1998), pp. 169–82.

7 David Clark, *Urban World/Global City* (Routledge, 1996), p. 190f.

8　On pages 14 and 15 of the Urban White Paper, *Our Towns and Cities: The Future* (DETR, 2000) this subtle shift of definition is implicit in the charts and text but never explicit, whereas the 1991 Census, from which the document draws its data, is quite clear.

9　The California School of Urban Geography (see, for example, Edward Soja, *Thirdspace: Journeys to Los Angeles and Other Real-and-Imagined Places* (Blackwell, 1996)) has moved our thinking from deterministic to more fluid understandings of the processes shaping urban landscapes and cultures.

10　United Nations *World Investment Report 1997* states that TNCs account for fifty-one of the world's hundred largest economic entities. The other forty-nine are countries.

11　Douglas Daft, quoted by John Lloyd in the *New Statesman*, 18 September 2000.

12　David Harvey, *Spaces of Hope* (Edinburgh University Press, 2000), p. 54.

13　R. Potter and S. Lloyd-Evans, *The City in the Developing World* (Longman, 1998).

14　See *Developments – the International Development Magazine*, Issue 10 (Department for International Development, 2000).

15　Moltmann, *Passion*.

3. The Story of Urban Mission

1　The history is recorded in *A Thing Called Aston: An Experiment in Reflective Learning* by Norman Todd, Michael Allen, Laurie Green and Donald Tytler (Church House Publishing, 1987).

2　Stephen Verney, *People and Cities* (Fontana, 1969).

3　Paulo Freire, *The Pedagogy of the Oppressed* (Penguin, 1972).

4　José Marins, T. M. Trevisan and Carolee Chanona, *The Church From the Roots: Basic Ecclesial Communities* (CAFOD, 1989).

5　Malcolm Grundy, *Light in the City* (Canterbury Press, 1990).

6　See *Challenging Communities: Church Related Community Development and Neighbourhood Renewal* by Doreen Finneron, Laurie Green, Sue Harley and Jim Robertson (Churches Community Work Alliance and Church Urban Fund, 2001).

7　*Faith in the City* (Church House Publishing, 1985), p. 74 explicitly names four criteria, but later chapters concentrate only on the first three criteria.

8　Austin Smith, *Journeying with God: Paradigms of Power and Powerlessness* (Sheed and Ward, 1990), p. 116.

4. The New Urban Challenge

1　See Andrew Davey, *Urban Christianity and Global Order* (SPCK, 2001).

2　Ash Amin, Doreen Massey and Nigel Thrift, *Cities for the Many Not the Few* (The Policy Press, 2000), p. 45.

3　*The Global Gamblers: British Banks and the Foreign Exchange Game* (War on Want, 1999).

4　See Ash Amin and Nigel Thrift, *Cities: Reimagining the Urban* (Blackwell and Polity Press, 2002).

5   United Nations Centre for Human Settlements, *Cities in a Globalizing World: Global Report on Human Settlements 2001* (Earthscan, 2001), ch. 1.
6   Saskia Sassen, *The Global City: New York, London, Tokyo* (Princeton University Press, 2001), p. 334.
7   Benjamin Barber, *Jihad vs. McWorld* (*The Atlantic Monthly*, 1992).
8   T. Butler and G. Robinson (University of East London) <http://cwis.livjm.ac.uk/cities>
9   Leech, *Through Our Long Exile*, p. 107.

5. Urban Meanings

1   See Jonathan Rabin, *Soft City* (Hamish Hamilton, 1974).
2   Leech, *Through Our Long Exile: Contextual Theology and the Urban Experience* (Darton, Longman & Todd, 2001), pp. 136–7.
3   J. K. Galbraith, quoted by John Madeley in *Hungry for Trade: How the Poor Pay for Free Trade* (Zed Books, 2001).
4   See Andrew Davey, *Urban Christianity and Global Order* (SPCK, 2001), p. 39.
5   Antonio Gramsci, *Selections from the Prison Notebooks,* ed. and tr. Quintin Hoare and G. N. Smith (Lawrence and Wishart, 1971). For a fuller discussion see my doctoral thesis, *In the Face of Domination* (New York Theological Seminary, 1982), pp. 417ff.
6   Quoted by Leech in *Through Our Long Exile*, p. 209.

6. Jesus, His Mission and His Praxis

1   Stanley Hauerwas, *The Peaceable Kingdom: A Primer in Christian Ethics* (University of Notre Dame, 1983, SCM edition), p. 113.
2   Bruce Chilton and J. I. H. McDonald, *Jesus and the Ethics of the Kingdom* (SPCK, 1987), p. 20.
3   Michel de Certeau, *The Practice of Everyday Life,* tr. Steven Rendall (University of California Press, 1992).
4   Juvenal, cited in R. H. Worth, *The Seven Cities of the Apocalypse and Roman Culture* (Paulist, 1999), p. 41.
5   John D. Crossan and Jonathan L. Reed, *Excavating Jesus: Beneath the Stones, Behind the Texts* (SPCK, 2001), p. xviii.
6   See Marianne Sawicki, *Crossing Galilee: Architectures of Contact in the Occupied Land of Jesus* (Trinity Press, 2000), ch. 9.
7   William R. Herzog II, *Jesus, Justice and the Reign of God* (John Knox Press, 2000), pp. 70, 98.

7. The Marks of the Kingdom

1   Martin Wallace, *City Prayers* (Canterbury Press, 1994).
2   Paul Spicker, *Poverty and the Welfare State: Dispelling the Myths* (Robert Gordon University, Aberdeen: Catalyst Working Papers, 2002).
3   See Laurie Green, 'The Body: Physicality in the UPA', in *God in the City,* ed. P. Sedgwick (Mowbray, 1995).

4   Richard Rogers and Anne Powers, *Cities for a Small Country* (Faber and Faber, 2000), p. 26.

5   See Mark Greene, *Supporting Christians at Work* (Administry, 2001).

6   Michael Safier, 'Confronting "Urbicide": Crimes against humanity, civility and diversity and the case for a civic cosmopolitan response to the attack on New York', in *City* (Vol. 5, No. 3, 2001).

7   *Community Cohesion: A Report of the Independent Review Team Chaired by Ted Cantle* (Home Office, 2001).

8   Christopher Duraisingh, 'Towards a Postcolonial Re-visionary of the Church's Faith, Witness and Communion', in *Beyond Colonial Anglicanism*, eds Ian Douglas and Kwok Pui-Lan (Church Publishing Inc., 2001).

9   Rogers and Powers, *Cities for a Small Country*, p. 44.

8. Street-level Ministry

1   Ivan Illich, *Disabling Professions* (Open Forum, Marion Boyars Ltd, 1977).

2   Anthony G. Pappas, *Entering the World of the Small Church – a Guide for Leaders* (Alban Institute Papers, 1988).

3   Charles Handy, *Understanding Voluntary Organizations* (Penguin Books, 1988).

9. Moving into Urban Mission

1   David Ford and Alistair McFadyen, 'Praise', in *God in the City* (Mowbray, 1995).

2   *A Fresh Start: Improving Literacy and Numeracy*, report chaired by Sir Claus Moser (DfEE, 1999).

3   *DIY Kit for Estate Ministry and Outreach* (available from 4 Chapel Court, Borough High Street, London SE1 1HW).

4   Joe Hasler, *Mind, Body and Estates: Outer Estate Ministry and Working Class Culture* (National Estate Churches Network, Church House, London SW1P 3NZ, 2000).

5   Laurie Green, *The Impact of the Global: An Urban Theology* (BSR, Church House, Great Smith Street, London SW1P 3NZ); Andrew Davey, *Urban Christianity and Global Order* (SPCK, 2001).

6   United Nations Centre for Human Settlements, *Cities in a Globalizing World: Global Report on Human Settlements 2001* (Earthscan, 2001).

7   Samuel Wells, *Community-led Estate Regeneration and the Local Church* (Grove Booklets, 2003).

8   George Barlow, 'New Approaches to Regeneration' (QMW Public Policy Seminar, April 1997).

10. Wider Horizons

1   The Anglican Urban Network produces a newsletter and runs seminars and research projects. Contact Andrew Davey, Church House, Great Smith Street, London SW1P 3NZ.

2   *Times Atlas of the World* (Times Books, 1997).

Additional Reading and Resources

Besides those specifically mentioned in the text, the following may prove helpful.

Bible

Crossan, J. and Reed, J., *Excavating Jesus: Beneath the Stones, Behind the Texts* (SPCK, 2001).

Herzog, William, *Jesus, Justice and the Reign of God* (John Knox Press, 2000).

Horsley, R. and Silberman, N., *The Message and the Kingdom: How Jesus and Paul Ignited a Revolution and Transformed the Ancient World* (Grosset/Putnam, 1997).

Logan, Pat, *The Centrality of the Kingdom of God in the Gospel* (Southwark Diocesan OLM Scheme, 2002).

Meeks, Wayne, *The First Urban Christians* (Yale University Press, 1983).

Urban mission

Ahern, Geoffrey and Davie, Grace, *Inner City God: The Nature of Belief in the Inner City* (Hodder & Stoughton, 1987).

Bosch, David, *Transforming Mission: Paradigm Shifts in the Theology of Mission* (Orbis, 1991).

Bradbury, Nicholas, *City of God? Pastoral Care in the Inner City* (SPCK, 1989).

Finneron, Doreen; Green, Laurie; Harley, Sue; and Robertson, Jim, *Challenging Communities: Church Related Community Development and Neighbourhood Renewal* (CCWA and CUF, 2001).

Green, Laurie, *The Challenge of the Estates: Strategies and Theology for Housing Estates Ministry* (National Estates Churches Network, 1999).

Green, Laurie, *Power to the Powerless* (Marshall Pickering, 1987).

Hazlehurst, Benny and Chapman, Chris, *The DIY Kit for Estate Ministry and Outreach* (available from 4 Chapel Court, Borough High Street, London SE1 1HW).

Holland, J. and Henriot, P., *Social Analysis: Linking Faith and Justice* (Orbis/Center of Concern, 1983).

Hunter, John, *A Touch of Class: Issues of Urban Mission* (Unlock, 1999).

Mander, J. and Goldsmith, E. (eds), *The Case Against the Global Economy* (Sierra Club Books, 1996).

Morisy, Ann, *Beyond the Good Samaritan: Community Ministry and Mission* (Mowbray, 1997).

Proctor, Keith (ed.), *Community Led Estate Regeneration Handbook* (CNHC, 2000).

Smith, Greg, *The Christ of the Barking Road* (October 1999). Greg's research will be found at <www.astoncharities.org.uk/research/gregsmith.shtml>.

Verney, Stephen, *People and Cities* (Fontana, 1969).

Vincent, John, *Hope from the City* (Epworth, 2000).

Wilkinson, J., *Church in Black and White* (Saint Andrew Press, 1993).

Faiths, Hope and Participation: Celebrating Faith Groups' Role in Neighbourhood Renewal (New Economic Foundation and CUF, 2001).

Faith in the City: A Call for Action by Church and Nation (Church House Publishing, 1985).

Global Civil Society 2001 (OUP, 2001).

Urban studies

Amin, A., Massey, D. and Thrift, M., *Cities for the Many Not the Few* (The Policy Press, 2000).

Bridge, G. and Watson, S., *The Blackwell City Reader* (Blackwell, 2002).

Bridge, G. and Watson, S., *A Companion to the City* (Blackwell, 2000).

Clark, David, *Urban World/Global City* (Routledge, 1996).

Davey, Andrew, *Urban Christianity and Global Order* (SPCK, 2001).

Harvey, David, *Spaces of Hope* (Edinburgh University Press, 2000).

Jones, Terence, *Britain's Ethnic Minorities* (Policy Studies Institute, 1996).

Koolhaas, Rem (ed.), *Mutations: Harvard Project on the City* (Actar Editorial, 2001).

Rogers, R. and Powers, A., *Cities for a Small Country* (Faber & Faber, 2000).

Sandercock, Leonie, *Towards Cosmopolis: Planning for Multicultural Cities* (John Wiley & Sons, 1998).

Understanding Cities series. (The Open University, 1999):

    Massey, D., Allen, J. and Pile, S. (eds), *Understanding Cities: City Worlds*.

    Allen, J., Massey, D. and Pryke, M. (eds), *Unsettling Cities: Movement/Settlement*.

    Pile, S., Brook, C. and Mooney, G. (eds), *Unruly Cities? Order/Disorder*.

Ward, Graham, *Cities of God* (Routledge, 2000).

Cities in a Globalizing World: Global Report on Human Settlements 2001, United Nations Centre for Human Settlements (Habitat) (Earthscan, 2001).

Our Towns and Cities: The Future Delivering an Urban Renaissance (DETR, 2000).

Towards an Urban Renaissance, Urban Task Force report, chaired by Richard Rogers (DETR, 1999).

Urban theology

Bakke, Raymond, *A Theology as Big as the City* (InterVarsity Press, 1997).

Fraser, Ian, *Reinventing Theology as the People's Work* (Wild Goose Publications, 1988) .

Green, Laurie, *The Impact of the Global: An Urban Theology,* 2nd edition (BSR, Church House, Great Smith Street, London SW1P 3NZ). Also available from the author.

Green, Laurie, *Let's Do Theology* (Mowbray, 1990; Continuum, 2000).

Harvey, A. (ed.), *Theology in the City: A Theological Response to 'Faith in the City'* (SPCK, 1989).

Haslam, David, *Race for the Millennium* (Church House Publishing, 1996).

Leech, Kenneth, *Through our Long Exile: Contextual Theology and the Urban Experience* (Darton, Longman & Todd, 2001).

Murray, Stuart, *City Vision: A Biblical View* (Darton, Longman & Todd, 1990).

Northcott, Michael (ed.), *Urban Theology: A Reader* (Cassell, 1998).

Roland, Chris and Vincent, John (eds), *Gospel from the City: British Liberation Theology Series* (UTU, 1997).

Sedgwick, Peter (ed.), *God in the City: Essays and Reflections from the Archbishop of Canterbury's Urban Theology Group* (Mowbray, 1995).

Vincent, John, *Starting All Over Again: Hints of Jesus in the City* (WCC, 1981).

Other resources

Periodicals

CITY. Analysis of urban trends, culture, policy, etc. (Carfax Publishing, Basingstoke RG24 8PR).

Urban Bulletin (incorporating *City Cries*) 305 Cambridge Heath Road, London E2 9LH. <xpressanny@aol.com>.

Helpful contacts

Baptist Urban Group: Reverend Mark Janes, 02074764133.

Children in Urban Situations (CURBS): <www.curbsproject.org.uk>.

Christian Aid: <www.christian-aid.org.uk>.

Church Action on Poverty: <www.church-poverty.org.uk>.

Churches Commission for Racial Justice: <www.ctbi.org.uk>.

Churches Community Work Alliance: <www.ccwa.org.uk>.

Churches National Housing Coalition: <www.justhousing.co.uk>.

Church Urban Fund: <www.cuf.org.uk>.

Evangelical Coalition for Urban Mission: <xpressanny@aol.com>.

Frontier Youth Trust: <www.fyt.org.uk>.

Globalisation and World Cities Study Group: <www.lboro.ac.uk/gawc>.

Grant information: <www.volcomgrants.gov.uk>.

HM Government's Urban Policy Unit: <www.urban.odpm.gov.uk>.

Joseph Rowntree Foundation: <www.jrf.org.uk/home.asp>.

Jubilee Group: <www.anglocatholicsocialism.org/jubilee.html>.

Laurie Green: <www.bishoplauriegreen.com>.

Multifaith Network: <www.interfaith.org.uk>.

National Estate Churches Network: BSR, Church House, Great Smith Street, London SW1P 3NZ, 020 7898 1446, or contact Laurie Green, <www.bishoplauriegreen.com>.

National Tenants Resource Centre: <www.traffordhall.com/LINKS.html>.

Neighbourhood Renewal Unit: <www.neighbourhood.gov.uk>.

New Economics Foundation: <www.neweconomics.org>.

UK Urban Mission Congress: <www.jitc.org.uk/home.html>.

Unlock: <www.unlock-urban.org.uk>.

Urban Bishops' Panel of the Church of England: Church House, Great Smith Street, London SW1P 3NZ.

Urban Theology Unit: <www.utusheffield.fsnet.co.uk>.

URC Urban Support Group: Sandra Ackroyd, 020 8881 7733.

William Temple Foundation: 0161 249 2502, <www.wtf.org.uk>.

Index

CPSIA information can be obtained at www.ICGtesting.com
Printed in the USA
BVOW042224270613

324577BV00012B/286/P